Rescuing Your Spirit

RESCUING YOUR SPIRIT

When Third-Grade Morality Isn't Enough For Christians

John C. Friel, Ph.D.

Health Communications, Inc.
Deerfield Beach, Florida

John C. Friel, Ph.D.
Lifeworks
St. Paul, Minnesota

Library of Congress Cataloging-in-Publication Data

Friel, John C.
Rescuing your spirit: when third-grade morality isn't enough for Christians / John Friel.
p. cm.
Includes bibliographical references.
ISBN 1-55874-265-4
1. Mental health — Religious aspects — Christianity. 2. Spiritual life — Catholic authors. 3. Theology, Doctrinal — Popular works. 4. Friel, John C., 1947- . I. Title.
BT732.4.F75 1993
248.8'6 — dc20 92-38928
CIP

ISBN 1-55874-265-4
©1993 John C. Friel

All rights reserved. Printed in the United States of America. No part of this publication may be reproduced, stored in a retrieval system or transmitted in any form by any means, electronic, mechanical, photocopying, recording or otherwise without the written permission of the publisher.

Publisher: Health Communications, Inc.
3201 S.W. 15th Street
Deerfield Beach, FL 33442-8190

Cover design by Robert Cannata

DEDICATION

To all of us.

ACKNOWLEDGMENTS

I would like to thank all the people who have touched my life over the past 46 years. I want to thank the ones who gave me life, who supported my struggles and with whom I have struggled. I include here the people who taught me, those who tried to prevent me from learning and those who challenged me to go beyond where I imagined I could go.

Thanks also to my editor Barbara Nichols for her thoughtful suggestions and extreme good humor during the final days of working on this manuscript, to senior editor Marie Stilkind, to my copy-editor Kathleen Fox, to my publishers Peter Vegso and Gary Seidler for supporting my work, and to my brother Rich Friel for our stimulating theological discussions and his deep insights into the work of Karl Rahner.

I would especially like to thank my wife Linda Friel for her support, encouragement, inspiration and help in clarifying many of the ideas in this book; and my children

Kristin, Rebecca and David for turning out to be such fine young adults with values and integrity as well as awe and wonder about the universe.

CONTENTS

PREFACE

In Oliver Stone's film *Wall Street,* Michael Douglas, playing the role of Gordon Gekko, a heartless Wall Street financial genius, gives a captivating speech at a stockholders' meeting as he attempts a takeover of the corporation. In his speech, he says, "Greed . . . is good. Greed is right. Greed works."

On May 1, 1992, during the riots sparked by the announcement of the verdict in the trial of the Los Angeles police officers who had beaten him, Rodney King came forward in tears and pleaded to everyone in front of the television cameras, *"Can we all get along?"*

Where is the Christ in Christianity? As the world shrinks and we are forced to absorb vast amounts of information in seconds rather than months, I see many people confused and searching. Many of us call ourselves Christians but we do it with trepidation and angst. Our emotions tell us to act one way, our church leaders tell us another and then we read the Bible and see a third way. Overwhelmed, we fall back to what feel like positions of safety — early childhood beliefs that may be embedded in fear and pain. Or we reject all early childhood beliefs because of our outrage at perceived hypocrisy. Feeling disillusioned and betrayed, we reject Christianity out of hand.

This book is for all who call ourselves Christians or have ever called ourselves Christians. It is for those of us who are searching to find the "Christ" in Christianity. It is for those of us who feel like hating ourselves or others because we are scared or because we don't know any better. It is for those who want to keep improving, keep thinking, keep searching and keep challenging. It is for those of us who are willing to look anew at what Jesus Christ had to offer the world.

I wrote this book for people who are open to taking a look at their beliefs in hopes of strengthening their faith. I wrote it for people who struggle with Christianity but have not yet given up the struggle. I wrote it for people who have been hurt by their religious upbringing but who are still willing to try to separate the messages of Christianity from the people who gave them the messages.

I started writing this book in 1989 and then got sidetracked when my publisher asked me to write what became *The Grown-Up Man,* my book about men. When I began this book, it was initially in response to scores of requests over the previous eight years from other professionals who had heard Linda and me speak at various workshops around the U.S. and Canada. During complex trainings on family systems, child abuse, addictions or stress, we would mention briefly the confusion and pain that so many people were experiencing due to their religious beliefs. We would note the serious damage that befell children who grew up in rigidly religious families. We would also mention the increasing number of religious organizations — Catholic, Baptist and Episcopal, to name a few — that had hired us to work with their clergy. We were asked not just to educate them about family dysfunction, but also to work directly to help those clergy who were in serious emotional trouble in their own lives.

We have worked with priests who are alcoholic, who have sexually abused children, who became priests to avoid the pain of growing up or who were gay and didn't know how to handle that facet of their identities. We have worked with ministers who have had numerous sexual affairs with members of their congregations, betraying their sacred trust as ministers. We have worked with clergy who were in the throes of a crisis about their own faith.

When these professionals would come up to us after our talk was over, they would typically ask something like this:

> We see so much pain bound up in people's religious belief systems. Is there anything written on this topic that can help people sort out the craziness and abusiveness from the healthy religious experience?

We began to realize professionals were hungry for basic information about religious issues that they could use to help their clients' confusion.

I also began writing this book in response to requests from our clients and workshop participants. As Linda and I began talking about *Churchaholic Families* in the early 1980s, we noticed that one or two frightened, brave souls would come up to us at break time and with great difficulty ask us very personal questions about the subject. After a while it was more than just one or two. The kind of question that would come from these participants, usually asked with puzzlement and pain, was:

> Somehow, I know what you are saying is true. It's happening in my very own neighborhood and family. But why? I don't understand how or why a good Christian Dad or Mom could physically, emotionally or sexually abuse their

children. Or why a good Christian family could be so hateful to other people because of their differences. Why?

When people asked this second question, we felt deep empathy for their confusion and pain. Here we are, practicing a religion which says we should love our neighbor, forgive, tolerate and be understanding — and then we find ourselves wounding others or being wounded. It just doesn't make sense. It feels like such betrayal. How can this be happening?

By the beginning of the 1990s, we were being asked by many groups to spend a portion of each workshop on religious problems.

Despite the many abuses of religion occurring today, I believe we as a people have begun to respond to the crises of child abuse and neglect, racism, intolerance, poverty and hatred in some tentative but positive ways. In that sense I feel many people are ready to hear the messages conveyed in this book — that belief in Christianity does not give us license to control, manipulate, abuse or hate each other. Nor does our Christianity ask that we remain fearful of new knowledge or that we deny our own shortcomings.

In addition to looking at what is unhealthy about the way we practice Christianity in America, I have focused on healthy spirituality, healthy love, healthy child-rearing and healthy self-knowledge as they relate to Christianity. Although this book focuses on Christianity, much of it applies to all people, religious or not.

This book is also for the hundreds of people we meet each year who are struggling gallantly and courageously with their own abuse and abusiveness. They are struggling with the role of spirituality in their lives. They want to have spirituality but have been so spiritually damaged, manipulated and frightened that it is next to impossible for them to find any. I am writing this book to offer a ray of hope. Perhaps it will give a few people a new route to spirituality. I hope to uncover some of the bigotry that we have foisted upon each other over the centuries in the name of Christ, God and religion, so we can let go of our damage and rage and embrace a new, healthier notion of Christianity and spirituality.

In *The Critical Journey,* Janet Hagberg and Robert Guelich wrote that the pain from early religious experiences often keeps us from being religious as adults. To be spiritually whole we must heal those wounds so we can embrace our religious heritage again.

CHAPTER 1

My First Encounter With "Christian" Hatred

And this is the condemnation, that the light has come into the world, and men loved darkness rather than light, because their deeds were evil.

John 3:19

As I travel back through my own life, I remember one of the first times I was personally touched by the contradiction between a person's purported beliefs and his actions. In 1961 I was in the eighth grade, in a public school and was an Episcopalian, but my sister and brother were fast converting to Catholicism. I learned an awful lesson about Catholics, especially all-boy Catholic high school students, that year.

My eighth-grade teacher was a good and decent man who was slightly effeminate in mannerisms. He wasn't the best teacher we had in grammar school, but he certainly wasn't the worst either. We basically liked the guy.

He lived in San Francisco and commuted to the town where we went to school. Apparently the fact that a man is somewhat effeminate is enough for some people to believe that they can strip him of his human rights. A bunch of boys from a San Francisco Catholic high school beat up my eighth-grade teacher and left him on the streetcar tracks where he was run over and killed. My classmates and I were young, but not so young that we couldn't be outraged, disgusted and appalled.

When I went to the University of San Francisco four years later, I noticed some male students who were popular and appeared to be extremely confident, even cocky. For some reason they scared me a little. I attributed it to my own insecurities at first, but as I stood within earshot of them at the Student Union one day I finally heard which high school they came from. It was the same all-boy high school in San Francisco that my teacher's killers had come from. Looking back, I now realize some of these guys were homophobic, rageful and abusive. Their obvious popularity with their peers had made me believe that there was something wrong with me for fearing them instead of the other way around.

I struggled with that for a long time. It seemed as if there was a whole cult of young men who had been altar boys, who had become sexually repressed, who hated women, who went to all-boy high schools, who were macho and cruel and yet destined to become the successful leaders of tomorrow. Or that's how my mind connected it at the time. By then I, too, was a Catholic so I was doubly confused.

Even though I am a psychologist who specializes in working with survivors of abusive families, and even though I understand how these things can happen, I still flinch inside when I think about that teacher's death. It was so senseless and pointless. Killings by "nice middle-class kids" were unheard-of back then.

For me, there was only one good thing that came out of my teacher's death. In my struggle to make sense out of such a senseless act, I eventually had to ask myself what Christ would have done in that situation. The internal struggle was very good for me. Most internal struggles are. No matter how I framed it for myself, I simply could not see how Jesus Christ meant for us to hurt, beat or even kill people because they walk, talk or look a certain way.

I couldn't fathom how being a good Catholic boy gave one the license to kill certain people because of their mannerisms or lifestyles. But I kept seeing men like that become community and even church leaders. I didn't know what to make of it. In fact, what I did was internalize their shame by assuming there was something wrong with me, not because I disapproved of killing an innocent stranger, but because I wasn't manly enough to fit in with this kind of person.

You might think this example is extreme, that this doesn't happen anymore. That was 1961. This is 30 years later. In truth, I suspect it is happening more today than it was in 1961 for a number of reasons, including the economic stress of the current recession. Perhaps you'll counter with the argument that it's happening more today with gay people. After all, the eighth-grade teacher wasn't necessarily gay, he was just "slightly effeminate." But what's the difference? They thought he was gay. That's why they beat him up.

It's the 1990s now and I still can't find anywhere that Christ said we should go around hating people, beating up people, shaming people or killing people because they are foreign, domestic, tall, short, fat, thin, intellectually gifted, intellectually disabled, religious, atheistic, gay or anything else.

How far have we progressed in terms of human rights since 1961? Quite a way, actually, but we still have a way to go.

On July 26, 1992, here in sleepy, safe Minneapolis, Minnesota, five men

> . . . chased a man they thought was gay near Lake Calhoun Sunday afternoon and bashed his car with tire irons and steel pipes when he tried to escape. Witnesses said a group of about 15 men had been walking along the lake carrying baseball bats and tire irons and yelling: "The score is one-nothing, let's get the fags."

As I read that story in the *Minneapolis Star Tribune,* all I could think was that they surely couldn't have been Christians. Christians would never do anything like that.

CHAPTER 2

The Heights Of Spirit

The wind blows where it wishes, and you hear the sound of it, but cannot tell where it comes from and where it goes.

John 3:8

Joseph Campbell said, "Anyone who's had an experience of mystery knows that there is a dimension of the universe that is not that which is available to his senses." Spirituality by its very nature is difficult to pin down. When I think about it, I come up with phrases like "the life of the soul," "the breath of life," "the force that binds the universe together" and "life." Spirituality is about trust rather than control. It is about power, surrender, relationship, intimacy, care, hope and subtlety. It is the foundation for love. It is the joy in the universe. It gives life. It elevates us. It does not kill, stifle or choke. It does not hate. It is not the darkness. It does not deceive. It does not diminish. In *The Evolution Of Chastity,* Pierre Teilhard de Chardin wrote, "The depths we attribute to matter are no more than the reflection from the heights of spirit."

These are all quite vague and perhaps, rightly so. We human beings in America are especially needy for concrete, practical definitions and solutions to our problems. But let me try to pin the idea down just a little bit more before I begin my discussion of how I believe our spirituality develops.

A SAMPLING OF VIEWS ON SPIRIT AND SPIRITUALITY

Several years ago I was invited to do a training workshop on spirituality for the staff of St. Luke's Gordon Recovery Center in Sioux City, Iowa, during Halloween week. They had requested that I do some experiential work with the staff in addition to simply lecturing. I decided to start off the day with a brainstorming session in which the 40 or so participants would generate as many free association responses as they could to the word *spirit.* I began to put everyone's responses up on the flipchart. It turned out to be both fun and enlightening. They enthusiastically shouted out items on their lists. Some of the responses were serious, some were reverent, some were fun, some were funny and some were outrageous. They were all legitimate under the rules of brainstorming, of course.

Because it was Halloween, there were some associations to the word *spirit* that might not have come up at a different time of year, such as:

Pumpkin	Jack O'Lantern	Sleepy Hollow
Witches	Halloween	Goblins
Poltergeist	Sheet	Candy
Scary	Monsters	Ghosts

Then there were the associations that had to do with personal energy and spiritedness:

School Spirit	Enthusiasm	Energy
Creativity	Fun	Excitement
Spunk	Humor	Motivator
Superman	Pep Rally	Drive
Pride	Force	Charisma
Will To Live	Desire	Spirited Horse

Then there were the words and concepts we usually associate with God, religion and spirituality:

God	Holy	Mystical
Grace	Dignity	Light
Breath	Mystery	Oneness
Being	Birth	Love
Death	Faith	Invisible
Humility	Nature	Morality
Water	Willow	Music
Crystals	Hanukkah	Mohammed
Safety	Floating	Angels
Unknown	Fear	Power Source
Wisdom	Center	Transcend
Tapestry	Reverence	Forgiveness
Expansion	Certainty	Christmas
Easter	Dove	Serenity
Passover	Nuns	Priests
Temple	Enigma	Heaven
Church	Intimacy	Protection
Freedom	Life	Connectedness
Yahweh	Allah	Guide
Holy Spirit	Holy Ghost	Ancestors
Soul	Awe	Wonder

As you can see, the word "spirit" conjures up a host of meanings for different people. Most of us have a sense of what spirituality means, but we also have a difficult time explaining that sense. One common theme I see in people's understanding of spirit is its intangibility. Many of us think of spirit as something that can't be physically touched. It is elusive and ethereal in terms of our physical senses.

Spirit also seems to be connected with life and breath for many people. It is the part of us that is alive and distinguishes us from things that are not alive. For some, it also means the part of us that will endure even after our physical bodies have perished — for these people it is connected with immortality. Some people call this part of us the soul.

There is also a sense of pervasiveness when people think of spirit. We think of the unifying forces in the universe, or the forces which bind all human beings together. And some of us think of *being* and *light* when we speak of spirit, words that fit in both religious and scientific contexts.

The notion of spirit as relationship is also present for many of us. We think of ourselves as being connected to one another through our spirits. We speak of the spirit of someone being in our hearts even after that person dies. We refer to someone's spirit being contained in a building that she designed, in a book that he wrote or in a painting that she created.

For some of us, spirituality is an intellectual response to the world around us. It is an appreciation of the unexplainable in the universe. Karl Rahner speaks of spirit as the "unutterable mystery." For others spirituality is more of an emotional response — about care and love and concern for one another, as well as about the awe and wonder that many of us have about the universe. Many people simply equate spirit with love.

Spirituality strongly implies surrender. Having awe and wonder implies that there is more to the universe than we understand. Being able to surrender in appropriate situations is the mark of a truly spiritual person. To fight with life and make ourselves miserable because we can't have everything we want when we want it, is the sign of spiritual immaturity.

In other words, "spirit" and "spirituality" are concepts that have been in human vocabularies for thousands of years. They have great meaning for most of us. With these preliminary descriptions of spirit let's take a trip through human development to see how spirituality emerges from its vague beginnings in infancy.

HOW DOES SPIRITUALITY DEVELOP?

In The First Few Years

On the last page of his outstanding book, *The Spiritual Life Of Children,* Robert Coles refers to each of us as spiritual "wanderers" and "explorers." The last sentence of his book describes our search in elegant terms. "Yet how young we are when we start wondering about it all, the nature of the journey and of the final destination."

A baby is born into the world with one indisputable force already clearly at work — the powerful drive to exist. All of the baby's prewired reflexes immediately leap into play to spell survival. The baby automatically searches for nourishment and sucks. He cries when hungry or in pain. He craves contact and nurturing. He begins to form strong bonds with those whose job it is to keep him alive. Within weeks, the baby begins to display a natural curiosity and sense of delight and wonder about his tiny world. He is filled with glee at novelty in his environment — a mobile over his crib that jiggles when blown by a gentle breeze, a parent playing peek-a-boo.

At the same time, the baby is beginning to make connections between what he does and the effects of those actions. If a baby can make the mobile over his crib turn by shaking his foot, his glee becomes ecstasy. "I can have an impact on my world!" he must be saying to himself in some preverbal way. Thus the first signs of intelligence are showing up in our baby.

As he grows and becomes more competent in his world, he automatically picks up the language of his culture. This ability to use abstract symbols to represent the world is one of the most amazing human abilities that we possess. The older he becomes, the more abstract his language ability becomes. At first he is only able to use language to describe things. As he matures, he begins to use language to express concepts, thoughts and feelings. At this point, the baby is no longer a baby. He has become a young child.

While the baby has been learning cause-effect relationships between himself and the world, and while he has been learning to symbolize his outer and inner worlds, he has also been getting something from those around him. If the baby is growing up in a healthy family, he is learning that he indeed will survive because he is being cared for; the world, while scary at times, is basically a safe place to be. In other words, he is learning trust, which forms the later basis for mature intimacy. He is learning how to get along with others and how to get his own needs met in the context of a family of other, similar beings.

He is also learning about authority and power. The earliest "higher powers" that we experience are our parents and caregivers. If they treat us with love, compassion, care, structure and limits, then we learn that we don't have all the power but we can trust those who do. We learn where we fit in the universe. We learn that, as we grow and develop, we can begin to share in that power as long as we do so responsibly and with the same care and respect that is afforded us by our parents.

There is so much that our baby is learning in the first two or three years of life. So where does his spirit fit in here? Our baby's spirit is manifested in his first gasps for life-giving air. It is manifested in his excitement and enthusiasm about the new and wonderful world into which he has been born. You can see and hear his spirit as he squeals and giggles about the simplest things. You can see it as he cries and struggles with issues of his very survival — issues of hunger, loneliness, fear and hurt. His spirit shows up in the endless questions he asks about every little facet of his world. In other words, we see a child's spirit in his awe, his wonder, his excitement, his struggle to survive, his questions, his language, his symbolism, his humor, his bonding with us, his love, his primitive empathy, his anger, his fear, his shame, his hurt and in all of his other feelings.

In Childhood

As our child grows, his ability to comprehend his world expands, too. He goes to school and learns, if he is lucky. As he learns, his tiny world of home and Dad and Mom starts to expand. He meets other children and bumps into their differing habits, customs and preferences. He learns how many things work. The school years are exciting for a healthy child who has healthy parents. It is a time of learning, discovering and wonderment. It is a time of mastery and increasing competence. It is a time when a child's spirit is manifested even more deeply through his feelings and his mind.

When a child first goes to school, it is scary and it is exciting. Remember this: the word "education" comes from the Latin "to lead out." True educators "lead children out" of the darkness and fear caused by ignorance and into the light of knowledge and understanding. A healthy parent will know that the child's goal is to begin living in a larger world that includes more than just Dad and Mom. His parents will therefore encourage him to form bonds with other adults and children. It is also a child's job to begin to understand more about the world, so his parents will encourage him and expect him to study, learn and think.

Through this process of learning about and bonding with other human beings, our child's ability to be spiritual increases because it increases his capacity for relationship. By learning more about the world through history, science, math, literature and so on, our child's ability to be spiritual deepens. This new knowledge lets him experience the mysteries and wonders of the universe while letting him know that "the more he knows, the less he knows." Thus, it lets him have more of that elusive awe and wonder about the universe that is such an integral part of being spiritual.

In Adolescence And Early Adulthood

During high school our child questions everything, including society's authority. He questions the existence of God, the teachings of his religion or nonreligion, the morals of his parents, right and wrong, lifestyles. He questions the whole ball of wax. As children grow into adolescence, the drive to expand and understand, explain and grasp, comprehend and question, and think and know gets even stronger. As Jean Piaget noted, adolescent idealism is an essential part of growing up. If it is squelched too early in the hopes of molding adolescents into a career or specific lifestyle, they will have a difficult time later in life ever realizing their true life goals.

The young adult's spirit is manifested in all of the earlier childhood modes. But now we also see our 25-year-old expressing his spirit in deepening intimacy with friends, associates and perhaps a mate. We see him wanting to have relationships with others out in the world in ways he was not capable of seven or eight years before. We see many young adults wanting to have children — wanting to maintain the human species on the planet. And we see them trying to make sense of their childhoods as they move deeper into adulthood. A young adult's spirit is now manifested in a larger connectedness with society and with his intimates. As he makes these connections with other humans, it is now possible for him to experience "spirituality" in the sense that many religious adults mean it.

In Summary: Where Does Spirituality Come From?

Spirituality comes from inside ourselves first, in its most primitive forms. It begins to deepen and mature as we learn more about and connect more with the world of people and things around us. As infants we experience trust and safety, as well as the thrill of discovering cause-effect relationships. As young children we learn to symbolize the worlds outside and inside of ourselves with language. We learn about the wonders of the universe. We continue to learn to trust those in authority over us as long as they don't abuse us. We begin learning to think. We begin learning to have emotional intimacy with others.

Our deepening ability to think allows us to comprehend the abstract. We need this ability to comprehend the abstract in order to have more than a four-year-old's concept of God. Our deepening emotional intimacy with other human beings lets us experience and become comfortable with deeper and deeper levels of intimacy in general, which is what a relationship with God is about. It stands to reason that if we can relate well to each other, we will have an easier time relating to our Higher Power. Relating to an unseen spirit or power isn't easy for us humans who are limited in certain ways by our physical bodies.

So our spirituality begins with and is made up of:

1. To Do — The Drive To Live And Survive

This includes our energy; our creative life force; our will; our desire to express ourselves and to make our mark on our world; our willingness to fight to survive physically, emotionally and spiritually; and our need to control our environment to protect our lives.

As we mature cognitively, our spirituality expands to include:

2. To Know — The Drive To Think, Comprehend And Understand

This includes our excitement about discovery of new things in the universe, from a mobile above our crib to the formation of the universe billions of years ago. It also includes the need to think, to question, to wonder and to hypothesize, even when this thinking or wondering leads us to ask questions that might frighten us or others. In *The Spirit In The Church,* theologian Karl Rahner stated, "We should consider human knowledge and freedom together, because in spite of the great differences between them, ultimately they have a common structure. In knowledge and freedom man becomes the very essence of transcendence."

It is my belief that the God in which I put my faith and trust wants me to think, wants me to improve myself, wants me to use my God-given talents and wants me to know and understand.

As we mature emotionally, our spirituality expands to include:

3. To Feel And Relate — The Drive To Connect With Self And Others And Therefore Be Intimate With Other Beings

This includes our desire to be close to others and to know and understand them while maintaining our own uniquenesss. It includes emotional intimacy and connection. This is frightening for many people, especially Americans, which partially explains why we seem to have so much trouble being authentically spiritual in this country.

Our spirituality, therefore, is not just about survival and developing our creative energies. It is not just learning about the mysteries of the world around us. And it is not just about relating to ourselves and others. It may begin with one of these, but if it is to deepen over our lifetime, it must include all three. No one knew this better than Jesus Christ who was the ultimate teacher, friend and active participant in His own world.

But What Does Spirituality Look Like?

Great thinkers and writers have tackled this question for thousands of years and I do not claim to have as much wisdom as they. But I do have my opinions, many of which I have learned from them during my own formal and experiential education. For Christians, Christ's life as described in the New Testament is the ultimate example of spirituality. But many people, Christian and non-Christian alike, say, "Yes, He was the Holiest of the Holy but He was also supposed to be God, so how can I even begin to be like Him?" Well, remember this: The whole point of the New Testament is that Christ was also *fully human.* This means each of us has the seeds of His kind of spirituality inside of us just waiting to grow.

Think about it. We are human. To be human means to be imperfect. We have flaws. This is what our healthy shame tells us. Our healthy shame asks us to be accountable for our mistakes, which is a less shaming way to speak of sin. We have feelings of hopelessness and despair. We get jealous. We get angry. These are not bad, they are simply part of being human. If you are a person who believes that Christ was both God and Man, then you must also believe that to be human is okay. Think about it.

If a human like Christ can be deeply spiritual, then we, too, can be spiritual. Perfectly spiritual? No. Remember, we're human. Okay. But what if I am so far away from that kind of spirituality and holiness that I feel defeated all the time? If I can't do it right and have it all, why even try? I feel like a failure all the time. I feel so insignificant compared to other people who are really on their way to being spiritual. This kind of thinking is very common among the clients in our psychology practice. It is called *all-or-none, black-and-white thinking.* It is also called *self-defeating thinking.*

I'll begin by telling you that I have never met a human being who has not had a spiritual experience, and I have never met a human being who does not have a core of spirituality inside of him or her. Karl Rahner also wrote that experience of the Spirit "*is* given to us, even though we usually overlook it in the pursuit of our everyday lives, and perhaps repress it and do not take it seriously enough."

I will also say that our American tendency to be competitive and individualistic makes it very hard for any of us to accept where we are in life without constantly comparing ourselves to the economic, social or even spiritual "achievements" of our neighbors. Because of our shame and fear of rejection in admitting realistically where we are in our personal development, we get paralyzed in denial and stay stuck so that we can't develop at all.

We could say, "This is where I am and these are my limits, so now I know where I am starting from." We say instead, "I have a vague hunch that I'm not as good as she is but I'd better not let myself or her know, because then I'll be a failure and she won't love me because nobody loves a failure." And maybe we're right. Maybe she doesn't love anyone she perceives as imperfect. But that's just an example of her flaws. Christ was very clear in His position on this one. He hung around with the dregs of society and found more holiness in many of them than He found in the self-righteous men of His day. Think about that one the next time you feel like a failure. And then look at your spiritual experiences.

Spirituality In Nature

When my brother, sister and I were kids, we would get our sleeping bags and sleep outside in the backyard on warm summer nights. We would look up at the clear, starlit-night sky for what seemed like hours on end. We'd watch for shooting stars and squeal with delight when we saw one. We'd wonder if there were other planets with people on them. We'd make up scary stories about Martians invading Earth. And somewhere between the laughter, the teasing, the stories and the temporary escape from the pain of our lives — sometime during those magical hours — I would feel totally insignificant and totally at one with the universe all in one eternal instant.

Spirituality In Church

Linda and I have clients who tell us they have searched and experimented with different churches, from the formal to the folksy and back again, until they have finally found a "good fit." Maybe it's just a different parish or congregation or synagogue. Or maybe it's a different religion altogether. They describe their church as being very comfortable and yet energizing, the way that truly happy couples describe their partnerships or marriages.

And every once in a while, for a brief but eternal instant, they tell us they will feel completely at one with all of the people at their church service and with all of humanity while feeling completely unique and separate at the same time. They are describing a spiritual experience.

Spirituality While Sharing Pain

When you have a painful secret that you have been holding inside of you, it begins to gnaw at your insides and isolate you from the companionship and acceptance of other humans. When you finally share that secret with other humans in a safe setting, as you might do in a therapy group or at a solemn family moment when everyone is open to taking the risk to share, the feeling is almost beyond description. There may be a flood of tears of relief at finally being unburdened and finally being seen and understood for who you are with all your flaws. There may be a flood of anger along with the tears, which is your way of saying, "I'm just a frightened child and I didn't deserve all of this pain." There may be a flood of shame and fear that you just exposed yourself and now you'll be hurt again. And then, if it's really a safe place, there will be an indescribable sense of peace and connectedness and acceptance among everyone in that room for one brief eternal moment.

Spirituality And Sexuality

For healthy people sex is sometimes serious, sometimes fun, sometimes gentle, sometimes wildly passionate and freeing, sometimes inventive, sometimes playful and sometimes just plain old comfortable. And sometimes, for one brief eternal moment, a sexual experience between two people who actually love each other produces a spiritual fusion of selves. This would be terrifying if the couple were not healthy and separate at the same time that they became "lost" in each other. Almost anyone can experience the fusion and apparent ecstasy of such encounters, but it is the dynamic tension between loss of self and keeping of self that lets two people experience the spiritual ecstasy of their sexuality. When you have felt particularly whole inside of yourself, when you have been able to cherish the dignity and fragility of your partner while cherishing your own dignity and fragility, and then the two of you have been able to merge your "selves" without losing your identity, then you have had a uniquely spiritual experience.

Spirituality And Good Works

Now let's look at Mother Teresa. She's a young nun riding on a train. She gets the idea that she's supposed to go to Calcutta and not just to help the poor but live with the poor. She's supposed to be poor. She's supposed to fuse with the poor but stay separate enough to do some good and not burn out or lose her sanity in the process. She's supposed to fight but be gentle, be strong but compassionate, be innocent but politically astute, work hard but not work herself to death, have joy amidst incredible sorrow, maintain her privacy but be with thousands, do it miraculously but remain humble and be vulnerable without being needy. In other words, she's supposed to cherish the fragility and dignity and power of the suffering souls in the gutters and alleys of Calcutta while cherishing her own fragility and dignity and power at the same time. That's spirituality in its simplest form — actions, thoughts and feelings.

Am I Kidding?

Yes, I know. The stuff about looking at the stars is something we can all relate to. And the stuff about being in church and feeling at one with humanity is within reach. Sharing the deep pain of your secrets with a group of people? Well, maybe someday. And this stuff about cherishing the dignity and fragility of yourself and your partner while sexually fusing but without losing your own self? "Well, that's beyond me," you might say.

"But Mother Teresa?" you ask. "That's a whole different story, isn't it? Nobody can be like Mother Teresa. She's totally unique." Think about that. It's a good example of absolute, black-and-white thinking. In truth, it is not a whole different story. It is exactly the same story. Every one of the examples above show individuals being spiritual. The innocent child looking at the stars, the adult sitting in church, the person sharing their pain, the couple celebrating their love sexually and Mother Teresa working in the streets of Calcutta are all examples of human beings struggling here on earth to be whole, to think and wonder and to connect with each other.

Jesus Christ spent time with and respected scholars, crooks, whores, tax collectors, kings, paupers, lepers, people suffering with mental illness, men, women, children, people who doubted Him, people who hated Him and people who feared Him. By doing that He told us that every last one of us is spiritual and has dignity. If you look at Mother Teresa and give up in despair because you can't be like her, it's because you aren't being human and you aren't being spiritual. If you look at the child's awe and wonder about the universe and say, "I had that once. I want to get it back," then you can join the human race and be spiritual, too.

Struggling And Waiting, Openly

I believe that part of being spiritual is our willingness to wait and be open to what is out there. Calvin Didier, pastor of House of Hope Presbyterian Church in St. Paul, Minnesota, gave an elegant sermon entitled "Spiritual Serendipity" one Sunday morning. The Bible quote that went along with it was from Luke 17:20. "The kingdom of God does not come while you are watching for it."

Pastor Didier told how Copernicus stumbled upon his revolutionary and quite correct view of the solar system when he was commissioned by the Church to determine on what day Easter should fall based on the phases of the moon. Little did he know what an uproar would ensue! How dare anyone say that our planet — and therefore *we* — were less central in the universe than people once thought? It took years for people to realize that just because we wanted to believe the sun rotated around us didn't make it so. It took many more years for people to realize that the more we learn about the universe, the more wonderful God's creation becomes for us.

Pastor Didier concluded his sermon by saying that letting go — spiritually — requires surrender and patience. Then he asked solemnly, "In our desperation to be saved, do we miss our chance for a deeper relationship with God?" On the cover of the church bulletin for that week was a quote from Eden Phillpotts: "The universe is full of magical things patiently waiting for our wits to grow sharper." In *Addiction And Grace,* Gerald May said, "Because grace is a pure gift, the most meaningful of our encounters with it will probably come at unintended times, when we are caught off guard."

In *Jesus: A New Vision,* Marcus Borg commented on the fact of Christ's freedom from fear, which he said was "grounded in the Spirit." And it is this grounding that allowed Him to have "courage, insight, joy and, above all, compassion." So as you contemplate your own spiritual development, remember that spirituality requires a paradoxical blend of struggle and patient waiting. Also remember what Christ taught us by His actions:

- None of us is perfect yet.
- We can't start growing again until we admit where we are now.
- We have to take risks to be spiritual.
- We have to think to be spiritual.
- We have to feel to be spiritual.
- We have to surrender to be spiritual.
- We have to wait patiently, openly but actively, to be spiritual.

CHAPTER 3

In The Beginning

In the beginning God created the heavens and the earth. The earth was without form and void; and darkness was on the face of the deep. And the Spirit of God was hovering over the face of the waters.

Genesis 1:1-2

Human history began with fear and pain, want and need and striving for survival. This is not a profound statement, it is just one that we too easily forget amid our hurried lives. In his posthumously published *Escape From Evil*, Pulitzer Prize winner Ernest Becker wrote: "But it is one thing to say that man is not human because he is a vicious animal, and another to say that it is because he is a frightened creature who tries to secure a victory over his limitations."

As a human being who works daily with other human beings who hurt, I am constantly reminded of how similar we all are. And we are not all that different from our primitive ancestors who survived on the planet without the aid of fax machines, cellular telephones and air conditioners.

How It All Started

For a brief moment, take a walk back in time with me to see what it must have been like for the earliest humans. Picture yourself living thousands of years ago when human beings first walked the earth. My clan lives in this valley. Your clan lives in that valley. We have a primitive language. The struggle for survival haunts us every moment of the day and night.

Because human beings have innate curiosity and wonder, one day you decide to see what's over the mountain in the next valley. More food, perhaps? Cleaner water? More wood for building fires? Animals with thicker fur to keep your family warm? You muster up all the courage you can, you gather some meager supplies and you begin climbing. After many days of cold at night and heat during the day, you get to the other side. You wander down off the mountain toward my valley. You cross a peaceful stream, and then our eyes meet. You are not of my clan and I am not of yours.

The first reaction we both have is *fear.* I grunt at you and you grunt back. I make threatening gestures and you gesture back. I fear that you will try to kill me and you fear that I will try to kill you. I worry that you will try to take away my food and my animal furs. I am afraid you will bring others and take my valley away from me.

There we are — two human beings face-to-face with each other — caught in the throes of a dilemma that has plagued us for thousands of years. Do I hate and conquer? Or do I love and cooperate? At that seminal moment, the march of history began. It has been a drama of antagonism, fear, cooperation, hate and love that always returns to the ultimate question: *"How will I survive?"*

In *The Duality of Human Existence,* sociologist David Bakan wrote that there are two competing themes in all of human affairs. One is the drive for separateness and the other is the drive for community. Bakan termed these two themes *agency* and *communion.* Both are essential for the survival of the human race. My need for *agency* tells me to come back to your valley with more of my clan so we can kill you or drive you off, leaving our clan with more resources. My need for *communion* tells me to approach you carefully and gently, to make friends with you, to form an alliance with you, to gain your trust, to meet the rest of your clan. Then I can return to my valley in the hopes of joining our two clans so we have more shared human resources for our mutual benefit and survival.

Our collective history can be framed as a struggle to balance these two competing themes. We need our separateness and uniqueness but in order to survive we also need each other. I believe that human beings are innately wired to care about each other. We don't always do it well. Sometimes we don't do it at all, but I believe the capacity to care is there.

So there we are thousands of years ago, you in your valley and me in mine. We mind our own business until our natural curiosity or our need for life-sustaining natural resources prompts us to travel beyond our little piece of earth. We run into each other and then off we go. I destroy you, then you come back and destroy me. Back and forth across the face of the planet we go, conquering and destroying and stealing from each other.

Pick up any world history book and you will read about the struggle of power, domination, empire-building, the rise and fall of cultures and the rise and fall of great leaders and belief systems. Six thousand years ago large cities began to emerge in Egypt and Mesopotamia. Five thousand years ago these same cultures unified around kings and queens who built massive public structures, such as canals, pyramids and palaces. Four thousand years ago "barbarians" — foreigners — began to invade, influence and in some cases weaken those existing empires. Egypt began to decline. Around 1600 B.C. the Hittites, Assyrians and Egyptians put together huge armies so they could spread their influence and their empires. The Jews and Phoenicians developed stable, peaceful cultures supported by trade 3,000 years ago. And 2,000 years ago Jesus Christ was born.

From Christ's time until this very day history has been one long continuation of empire-building, invasions, wars, consolidation, decline, fragmentation and rebuilding. The Roman Empire, which once extended from Egypt all the way to the British Isles, fell in 476 A.D. As we look at our history books, we read of the "barbarians" again — of the Visigoths, the Ostrogoths, the Vandals, the Franks, the Lombards, the Muslims, the Vikings and the Magyars. They pillaged and plundered and fought and conquered across Europe and the Middle East. Then a more consolidated Europe, centered around the Catholic Church, began to fight back. Genghis Khan formed the Mongol Empire in China. On and on we've gone. The breakup of the Soviet Union and all of the bloodshed and battles over turf are not new. Peace is something that is new, where it exists at all.

If that were all we'd been doing for the past 100,000 years, we'd be pretty sorry beings.

Cultures

But it isn't all that we've been doing. Our need for communion also prompted us to form larger and larger groups. We began to form rules for belonging to the group which we believed were necessary for our survival on the planet. So we had rules about which foods were safe to eat and which were not. We had rules about who could have sex with whom. Almost all of us had rules or taboos against incest. We had rules about keeping the fires going so we wouldn't have to go through the arduous process of restarting them all the time. In other words, while we were doing all of this stealing and conquering, we were also developing cultures.

Down through the generations people developed an understanding about the world and about life. Then they passed these accumulated understandings on to their children in the hope that their children could survive in the world and make sense of their lives, too. As fathers and mothers here and there shared their common understandings about life, communities formed and cultures developed. A simple way to explain a "culture" is to say that it is the shared survival mechanisms, understandings and meaning systems of a group of people on the planet. Our culture is defined by how we survive, what we believe, how we find meaning in life and how we celebrate all of the above.

In some cultures people survive by producing food in huge quantities and then shipping it around the land by truck or train. They pass information back and forth to one another via computers, telephones and fax machines. In other cultures people survive by foraging for food in the jungle. They pass information back and forth via drum beats. Some people celebrate the meaning of life with colorful costumes and dances. Others do so by wearing rather drab costumes and sitting quietly in rows inside of big buildings.

In some cultures music is controlled and mathematical. In others it is free and spontaneous. Some languages have a tight, controlled quality to them, while others have a flow that is sensuous and open. In some cultures anger is expressed directly and freely. In others it is rarely expressed at all. Some people believe in a personal creator, some believe in a unitary force and some believe in fate. Some people give meaning to life with all of its mysteries by believing there is life after death. Others believe that the meaning of life is in the living. Still others believe there is no meaning in life at all.

The Egyptian culture of 5,000 years ago had music, art, poetry and a proliferation of gods that allowed rulers of cities and kingdoms to legitimize their power. Approximately 2,900 years ago, as the Greek Empire came to power, there was a culture-wide consolidation of thinking in science and in the arts that formed the basis of most of our thinking today. The period from 500 B.C. to 300 B.C. gave us Sophocles, Euripides, Aristotle, Plato, Socrates, Hippocrates, and yes, even Epicurus who suggested that the only reason for living was pleasure.

Around the world other great cultures and belief systems were developing at the same time. The Mayans of Central America began their civilization. In India, Siddhartha Gautama founded Buddhism, a peaceful system of thought and living that proposed nonviolence and meditation. The Native Americans in what is now the United States established themselves in permanent villages, began formal agricultural experimentation and also had religious and political leaders.

Cultures Under Stress

When people are afraid or in pain, they sometimes do things to hurt themselves or others. While our cultures are designed to help us cope with day-to-day living, life sometimes throws us a curve that we aren't expecting and that our culture is ill-prepared to handle. When certain tragedies hit us, something seems to break down. Perhaps it is our trust that gives way first. We no longer fully believe what our culture has taught us. The meanings that we have attached to life get shaky. We fear for our very survival. Then we do things that we ordinarily wouldn't do. If our leaders get too scared, they will lead us to do things we ordinarily wouldn't do.

Leadership

Agentic Leadership

As primitive people joined together into social-survival groups, it became clear that leadership was necessary. Someone had to be invested with the power to make decisions for the group as a whole to ensure their survival. In most of our elementary schools we learn primarily about the political leaders and conquerors who used military force to unite peoples and to destroy others. We speak of many of these leaders as barbarians. Yet leaders who were most concerned with politics and building empires served an important purpose. Whether they meant to or not, they unified large groups of people and allowed cultures to develop. They were concerned about resources and therefore survival. As we populated the planet and struggled with our solutions for survival, leaders emerged who raped, pillaged, conquered, unified peoples and built empires. These political leaders seemed to be concerned with survival in its most raw, biological forms. People were enslaved and children were routinely killed or abused. Having power meant taking whatever one wanted regardless of the human consequences.

Communal, Spiritual Leaders

Different kinds of leaders emerged as well because human beings have other needs. We have a need to know and understand. We have a need to care for each other. We have a need to understand the awesome secrets of nature. We have a need to be spiritual and connected with the universe. And we need systems of meaning that can help us treat each other humanely when we are under stress.

These communal leaders were men and women who struggled with the meaning of life and with what constituted the common good. They were people who created works of art and music to symbolize and express the feelings and deeper experiences of the culture. They were spiritual people who looked past mere biological survival and who allowed the human need to care for others to emerge in themselves. These leaders tried to provide the communal perspective that humans need to survive on the planet. Agentic leaders know intuitively that people who care but who can't get anything done will not survive. Communal leaders know intuitively that leadership without human care will mean the end of the human race.

What began to emerge on the planet were systems of belief that helped people make sense out of the confusing and unknown, and eventually led to more humane treatment of people. The Greeks and Romans created gods to explain natural phenomena such as the movement of the planets and changes in the weather. These belief systems also gave people a code of behavior to guide them in stressful and confusing situations.

As Mortimer Adler noted in *Truth In Religion,* religion helps us come to grips with "Mankind's sense of its delinquency and the inadequacy of its own powers to raise itself up above where it finds itself." Human beings came to realize that they needed moral guidance and principles of living to help them survive. At some point in history we humans, in our various cultures, must have connected inside with our innate need for justice and mutual care. At that point we were ready to listen more carefully to our communal leaders. In Judeo-Christian history Moses was such a spiritual leader.

According to the Old Testament we began to look for deeper meaning in life. We struggled to know our Creator. We wrestled with good and evil, with the notion of an afterlife and with the place of rules and regulations in guiding the daily conduct of men and women. The Ten Commandments gave us a set of rules that were not simply political — they were moral, emotional, spiritual and communal.

Slowly, over time, those rules and regulations were gathered together into what Wilfred Smith defined as *religion* — that is, "cumulative traditions" which constituted the faith of the people in a culture. Over the centuries we started to get lost in ourselves and in all of those rules. We tried to "live by the book" but forgot the underlying reason for the book. We made the rules more important than their meaning. We put ashes on our faces to make it appear as if we had been fasting, believing that appearances must be everything. Many of us became artificial and false.

Two thousand years ago, according to Christian belief, a Man appeared on the scene to try to get us back on track. He lived a very simple life, said some very simple yet powerful things, and wound up being hated, persecuted and eventually killed. But He left us with some simple wisdom that is still around today if we look carefully enough. The problem is that it's been 2,000 years since this Man died and over the centuries we humans have done the same thing we've done with the teachings of other great spiritual leaders throughout history. We've blurred the original message.

In This Century

Now in the late 20th century pick up a newspaper or a national newsmagazine and read the headlines. What do you see? I see stories about the struggles of human beings to make sense of their lives. I see broad political dramas of nations in turmoil; of races and cultures striving for security, peace and dignity; of individuals caught up in personal scandals. As I read more carefully, I see people who are frightened that their children won't have enough to eat. I see people who are afraid their neighbors or neighboring countries will invade them and take away their freedom. I see homeless people in rich nations being treated like so much debris. I see women, foreigners, people of color, people of different races or religions being treated like slaves.

For many years sociologists have noted that whenever a society gets too stressed, it looks for people to blame. We call these people "scapegoats." Whenever a culture gets too stressed or too greedy, somebody has to pay. During the Great Depression hate groups flourished all over the world. Here in the United States the Ku Klux Klan had a field day. Now with economic hard times upon us around the world again, the same is true. We're on the prowl, looking for scapegoats.

We don't start out hateful and vindictive. We start out being scared. We see the fear or hunger or uncertainty in the eyes of our loved ones and we ache inside. We believe that we can survive but we aren't sure how. The stress builds. Our anxiety deepens. A job is lost here, an uninsured medical crisis happens there and we begin to sink. We look for answers but our leaders don't have any. Something is wrong somewhere. We squirm and struggle some more. We long for leadership, for someone to define the problem, to give us clarity, direction and renewed hope. We aren't ignorant. We're scared.

Someone with charisma appears. We want to believe. We want him to take away our pain. We long for answers, the simpler the better because now we're starting to go under. We begin to lose our values. We begin to lose our identities. We begin to lose our hope. We give ourselves away. We give the leader our money, our dignity and our humanity. Then we give him our beliefs. Finally, and worst of all, we give him our children.

This is what happened in Nazi Germany. But it has happened many other places, too. It happened in the killing fields of Cambodia, with apartheid in South Africa, in America with Native Americans and African-Americans.

It has happened all over. It happens every time a man beats his wife or children "in the name of God." It happens every time a woman abandons her children for the sake of an unhealthy relationship. It happens when we as parents teach our children to hate and fear people who are different "because God says people who are different are evil." It happens when young men from "nice homes" rape their female classmates at college and laugh about it the next day, then blame it on the victim. It happens when we fill our homes with guns so that we as a "wealthy" industrialized nation have one of the worst rates of violent crime in the "civilized" world.

Yes, when we get stressed enough about our own survival, something happens. We lose our care and concern. We worry about our own. We begin to hate. We take what isn't ours. We create new meaning and belief systems that justify our insensitivity and abuse of others. We lose sight of our values. We begin to destroy or kill. And then we take two steps backwards. One of the reasons I am writing this book is to remind myself about this because I am just as human as everyone else on earth.

Before we move on to the next chapter, I would like to state for the record some of the basic principles of families that operate on all of us and can powerfully affect the way we treat each other in the world.

How It Works

The child is father of the man. Many scholars view world history optimistically and see that over the centuries our cultures have become healthier, more enlightened and more sensitive to human needs. I tend to believe this also, especially in light of some compelling historical evidence. But it is a painfully slow process because, as William Wordsworth wrote in 1807, "The child is father of the man."

Each generation of young people coming into adulthood faces a period of re-enacting their own childhood patterns. Survivors of child battering batter their own children until they get help. Or else they have trouble setting healthy limits for the children because they fear hurting their feelings, and thus they produce children who are spoiled. Spoiled children often grow up to be abusive or neglectful of their own children. So the process of pain gets passed down from one generation to the next.

But somehow we slowly improve. The rules and meaning systems in our cultures change and grow. More humane treatment of each other becomes part of our institutions so that more and more people treat each other with respect and care. Whether out of economic necessity and simple pragmatism, or because of a higher set of values, human beings have managed to come up with a Magna Carta and a Bill of Rights, to name two examples. Slowly? Yes. But it does show progress.

Each new generation is faced with the task of survival. Each new generation believes its elders and copies its elders' behavior. Each new generation is faced with stress. Each new generation hurts itself and others. Each new generation changes its culture and institutions. Each new generation hopes that the one after it can do better. Each new generation goes two steps forward and one backward.

Children believe their parents. When a father tells his children that some men kill each other, his children believe him. When a mother tells her children that Santa Claus brings them presents, her children believe her. That's how families operate. Children are dependent on parents and look up to them. Children need to learn from their parents. They want to learn from them. They do learn from them.

When a father tells his children that he is losing his job and that the family is in financial stress, his children believe him. You can tell that they believe him because they begin to worry about money and survival. They ask questions about it. They try to help in little ways. When a mother tells her children that Dad and Mom aren't getting along, that they are seeking marriage counseling to try to resolve their problems, her children believe her. You can tell they believe her because they worry a little more. They watch Dad and Mom a little more. They try to help in little ways. They may have signs of emotional stress in their young lives.

Yes, children believe their parents. When parents tell their children that Republicans or Democrats are stupid, their children believe them. When children are told that African-Americans are to be feared, they believe it. When they are told that women or men are bad, they believe it. When they are told that gay people should be exterminated, they believe it. When they are told that all poor people are just lazy, they believe it. When they are told that anger is bad, that joy is good, that it's shameful to be afraid, that vanilla ice cream is boring, they believe it. Children believe these things because it's part of survival for children to believe what they are told by adults. That's how it works.

Children do what their parents do. In truth, children don't believe everything we tell them. If I tell one of my daughters that the sky is green, she'll laugh and say, "Oh, you're just teasing me, Dad." If I tell my son that all Democrats or Republicans have horns and tails, he'll laugh and say, "C'mon, stop kidding around!" Children have eyes and ears and noses and tastebuds and they feel things when they are touched. They won't always believe what we say. But children do what we do.

If I tell my children that it's important to stand up for themselves, they may believe me at some level. But if I don't stand up for myself, they probably won't stand up for themselves either. Or else they'll go overboard in the other direction and stand up for themselves on every little issue until no one wants to be around them anymore. If I tell my children that exercise is good for them, they may believe me. But if I don't exercise regularly myself, they'll have a hard time following through with it on their own.

If I tell my children that a good person is tolerant of others and then complain about other people all the time, my children will learn to be intolerant of others. Then, when I get mad at them for being so intolerant, they will feel confused and betrayed inside but won't know why. The fact is that we don't have to be aware of our parents' behavior to copy it. We just copy it anyway. That's how it all works.

The Big Picture

According to the Gideon Bible, which is placed in hotel rooms throughout the world, there is one verse from the Bible that has been translated into more than 1100 languages and which is one of the most important verses in the New Testament. It states simply:

> For God so loved the world that He gave His only begotten Son, so that whoever believes in Him should not perish, but have everlasting life.
>
> John 3:16

By this one brief statement thousands of years of history and belief were rewritten and millions of people who would otherwise be hopeless suddenly had or would have hope. This is the essential message of Christianity — that we can be saved from ourselves and from our mistakes.

Please try to remember that we're all in this together. Despite our high technology and thousands of years of accumulated wisdom, we are still concerned with many of the same things that concerned our primitive ancestors. Remember, too, that despite all of our cultural, moral and technological advances, we're still afraid that the guy in the next valley will come over the mountain some day with all of his pals and wipe us off the face of the planet.

Lastly, if you are a Christian, please remember that Christ's message is quite simple. It is we who get the message confused.

CHAPTER 4

Hell On Earth: How Our Spirits Get Damaged

Assuredly, I say to you, inasmuch as you did it to one of the least of these My brethren, you did it to Me.
Matthew 25:40

IN THE NAME OF GOD!

"In the name of God, Bobby! What the hell's the matter with you?" The little boy in the supermarket looked startled first, then scared and finally ashamed. He didn't have an answer for his father, who was now embarrassed himself because he knew other people in the store had seen him treat his son this way. It was all over in a matter of moments. The son's minor infraction of grocery store decorum. The father's frazzled over-reaction. The son's shame; the father's shame.

Hopefully they would settle it before the father had the engine of the car running and they were on their way home. Perhaps Dad would apologize for snapping, which would remove the shame felt by the son. Then the son wouldn't have to remain defensive, so he could apologize to Dad. As Gershen Kaufman would put it, the bridge between father and son had a break in it which produced some shame. It could be repaired in this case fairly easily.

What interests me even more as a psychologist is the phrase "In the name of God!" We say things like this without even thinking because the phrases are a part of everyday vocabulary for many of us. But do we really mean that in the name of God we want Bobby to settle down? Is God sending us a private message about Bobby, that for His sake we need to tell Bobby to settle down? I rather doubt it. It sounds so silly when it's put that way, doesn't it?

We have many other phrases that we use unconsciously, too. When we curse, some of us say "God damn it!" Do we really want God to damn someone or something? A child is afraid to tell the truth about taking her brother's toy and some parents say "God will punish you for that lie!" Is that really the kind of stuff God focuses on?

Theologians and philosophers have grappled with the notion of sin and evil for centuries. More recently, anthropologists, sociologists, psychiatrists and psychologists have joined in the struggle. A 1991 cover of *Time* magazine stated: "EVIL — Does It Exist Or Do Bad Things Just Happen?" A 1991 cover of *U.S. News & World Report* said: "The Rekindling Of HELL — Record Numbers Of Americans Now Believe In A Netherworld And In A Wide Variety Of After-Death Punishments." I suspect there is a strong connection between this belief and people's growing sense of powerlessness, frustration and outrage about the underlying lack of justice in our society right now. If they aren't going to get caught on earth, at least they'll go to hell!

But far be it for me to try to tackle that subject. What I can share with you are some of the things I personally witness on a daily basis that I consider to be serious human mistakes that create hell for people right here on earth. Since they are human mistakes, I presume Jesus Christ would want us to take a look at them and then start correcting them, which is what forgiveness and redemption are all about. Forgiveness doesn't mean we say we're sorry and then keep doing it. It means we are human and are allowed to have room for error, but when we see the error of our ways, we are then invited and helped to change our ways.

WHERE IS HELL ON EARTH?

Clergy/Professional Helpers

At the end of the HBO film *Judgment,* which was a true story about the sexual abuse of boys by a Catholic priest, the statement was made that as a result of the case portrayed in the film, most insurance carriers will no longer insure the Catholic church for claims made due to the molestation of children by priests. Until a few years ago the painful truth of molestation of children by the clergy was denied by almost everyone. Even worse, it was deliberately and willfully covered up by the very high church authorities in whom the victims and their families had placed their sacred trust. A person with just a little bit of common sense, decency and compassion can easily understand how the sexual molestation of a child by a priest is spiritual abuse. But the fact of church officials covering up the abuse and protecting the offender is so reprehensible that we have a hard time even believing it.

Since I began this book, another sadly shocking case of massive sexual abuses of children has come to light, with every day bringing new allegations from survivors around the nation. Through the excruciatingly painful and courageous initial efforts of Frank Fitzpatrick, it was revealed that in the 1960s in Massachusetts, a charming young Catholic priest, Father James Porter, began molesting scores of children in his parish. In several cases, Father Annunciado, a priest in the same parish, stumbled onto Father Porter in the act of sexually abusing his victims. Father Annunciado simply shut the door and went away in silence.

This case was tastefully and compassionately presented by Diane Sawyer on *PrimeTime Live* in July of 1992. During that telecast I had the privilege of witnessing the horror, disgust, outrage, healing and love of the many survivors of Father Porter's abuses who chose to come forward and participate in the program. While it was painful to hear of the abuses, it was spiritually moving to see these honorable, courageous people support each other in their pain. It was true Christianity in action.

When the case first broke in the press, I was as horrified as anyone else, despite my familiarity with sexual abuse cases. But what really caught my eye and horrified me was the public reaction by Cardinal Bernard Law of Boston. He snapped into the news reporter's camera something to the effect that all the press was doing was making it hard on all of the good priests out there. His "official statement" quoted in the *Los Angeles Times* was that it was "the tragedy of a priest betraying the sacred trust of priestly service." But the cameras of *PrimeTime Live* showed Cardinal Law preaching from his pulpit, presumably at Mass, saying, "By all means, let's call down God's power on the media."

If I were a victim of sexual abuse and a Catholic, this remark from a high Church official in such an angry, accusatory tone would probably fool me into feeling ashamed of my outrage. I would probably nod in agreement, my eyes glazing over in the dissociation that goes with being abused. Then I would comfortably go back into denial about the horrors that these scores of adult children experienced and are still experiencing.

But that wasn't my reaction. My reaction was outrage. How dare he try to gloss over such an infinitely disgusting betrayal of children's faith and innocence by trying to dump the shame back onto those who have a duty to expose this kind of abuse! How dare high Church officials sit back and hope that it all blows over! How dare a bitter, frightened, angry old man of a Cardinal claim to be a representative of Jesus Christ! How dare he! It is true that one bad apple doesn't mean that the whole barrel is rotten, but Cardinal Law missed an incredible opportunity for accountability and healing — especially for the survivors of Father Porter's sexual atrocities.

What if Cardinal Law had said the following?

> What Father Porter did was atrocious. It never should have happened. There is no way that we can undo it, but as a representative of the Catholic Church I apologize from the depths of my soul for what a fellow clergyman did to you. I applaud the press for exposing these abuses so we can all know about them, so the survivors can feel believed and begin to heal, so we can increase our very early, tentative efforts to treat our priests who are sexual offenders.

If he had said that, he would have been a model of true Christianity. But he didn't. He chose to shame the victims indirectly by attempting to shame the press who were, by reporting these atrocities, allowing the victims to begin to be believed and heal. I pray that Cardinal Law is just another bad apple and that the Church as a whole takes its rightful place of spiritual and moral leadership for millions of Catholics before too much additional damage is done. Looking the other way is not what leaders or Christians do. In this case, looking away is so awful that we can hardly believe it ourselves. But we must not look away from those who looked away or we will be just as morally bankrupt.

As I considered the statement at the end of the HBO film, I told myself it is not particularly consoling to think that it may be purely economic factors that have forced many churches to struggle with the problem of abuse by the clergy. "Uh-oh! We got caught. No more insurance. Guess we'd better stop this child abuse stuff now." According to Jason Berry, author of *Lead Us Not Into Temptation,* a new book about pedophilia and the Catholic Church, 400 Catholic clergy have been reported for child sexual abuse in the past ten years, with a cost to the church of $400 million.

Are churches evil? No. The people in them are human. I know that. Sometimes we humans have to have our insanity stare us in the face before we're willing to look at it. If that awareness comes in the form of an insurance carrier, then so be it. And we should all be aware that many churches, including the American branch of the Catholic Church, are responding in very appropriate ways. After being hit especially hard by the Father Thomas Adamson child sexual abuse case here in Minnesota, the Archdiocese of St. Paul and Minneapolis instituted an extremely forward-looking program of help for and cooperation with abuse victims. The Vicar General, Rev. Kevin McDonough, stated in the *Minneapolis Star Tribune,* "We're looking at all the abuses of power, which could even be with adults or co-workers. We're trying to address and identify the needs of all the various parties involved."

In that same newspaper article it was noted that six Christian denominations have been leaders in dealing with sexual abuse by clergy in the state of Minnesota: the Evangelical Lutheran Church in America, the Roman Catholic Church, the United Church of Christ, the United Methodist Church, the Episcopal Church in America and the Presbyterian Church USA. In an article in the *Minnesota Psychologist,* Gary Schoener, Executive Director of the Walk-In Counseling Center in Minneapolis and a nationally recognized, competent, respected psychologist and expert on abuse of clients by professionals, noted that American churches have actually done a much better job of dealing with these kinds of abuses than have psychologists or psychiatrists. In looking at training materials provided by churches versus those by psychologists, Schoener wrote, "Very frankly what the clergy have available is far superior."

In a recent study conducted by psychiatrist Nanette Gartrell and published in the *Western Journal Of Medicine*, one in ten doctors reported having sexually abused their patients. Of these cases, 90% were between male doctor and female patient, 5% were homosexual and 6% were between female doctor and male patient. Commenting in the *Minneapolis Star Tribune* on how to deal with this problem, Gary Schoener stated, "We've tried one approach — the use of ethics codes. That hasn't worked. It's time to move to Plan B: criminalization, better functioning licensing boards, mandatory reporting, and aggressive public and professional education."

We must never forget that the sexual abuse of a child by anyone is horrible. The sexual abuse of a child by a parent, teacher, doctor, psychologist or the clergy is worse in my estimation because of the betrayal of the sacred relationship that is supposed to exist between children and these authority figures. The covering up of such abuse by the boards or councils who govern the activities of professionals is the closest thing to true evil that I can imagine.

Women

According to historical facts presented in Iowa State University educational materials on domestic assault and rape, the word "family" comes from the Latin word "familia" which refers to a group of slaves that belongs to a man. The authors point out: "In 2400 B.C. if a woman was verbally abusive to her husband, he engraved her name on a brick and knocked out her teeth with it." They also noted that between 200,000 and 900,000 rapes occur annually in the United States, and that 22,000 men are arrested for rape each year. "In at least 70% of the cases the victim knows her assailant," and a "large number of reported rapists are married, and most are less than 30 years of age." In trying to understand rape, they finally noted that, "The abuser's main motivation is not pent-up sexual desire, but aggression, domination and power."

In ancient Greece and Rome it was typical for only one female infant to be allowed to live because females were not valued. In the book of scholarly articles entitled *Abuse And Religion: When Praying Isn't Enough,* different authors point out that families at high risk for domestic assault and violence, as well as child abuse, are patriarchal families where there are both fear and hatred of women. The authors of these articles, who represent various religious faiths, all seem to concur that many people, both men and women, have misinterpreted the Bible to use it to justify abuse and hatred of women.

We can look back to 2400 B.C., shake our heads and say, "Tsk, tsk, tsk — my, but weren't they barbaric back then!" And then we can go about our day with the confidence of a people who have overcome barbarism. But have we? What will people 2,000 years from now say about us? I bet they will talk about how barbaric our treatment of women was. They will look at the Navy's Tailhook Association horror, in which women were sexually abused "all in good fun," as barbaric. They will look at the Anita Hill/Clarence Thomas hearings and shake their heads in dismay and disgust. They will look at pay inequities, domestic violence and marital rape in shock and disbelief.

What will they think of our handsome young college men who make it a sport to gang-rape a young college woman, videotape it and then laugh about it the next day?

This is such a common occurrence on college campuses in the United States of America that officials at these institutions have had to conduct special seminars and training to help them/their staff/school officials deal with the problem. What will they think of our fear and hatred of women, and of our deeply ingrained belief that women are responsible for their own rapes? If it were any issue other than a sexual one, we would be outraged today. The prevailing mood says otherwise when it comes to women and sex.

Oh, yes, I understand it. Men have a stronger sex drive and are biologically set up to be "the pursuers" because of testosterone. Women are biologically set up to be more powerfully drawn to nurturing and care, and to be "the pursued." Okay, okay. I understand that women have been seen as having mysterious powers and mysterious biological goings-on inside of them which occasionally culminate in the birth of a human being. Men don't understand women and women don't understand men. None of these aforementioned "facts," however, gives one human being the right to abuse, berate, belittle, rape, rob, neglect, hurt, cheat or maim another human being. Men have been doing just that for centuries in the the name of God, Jesus Christ, Testosterone and Larger Muscle Mass, and it's time for us to stop.

Some people believe that God is actually an old man with a long white beard. Most people who believe that are around four years old, either chronologically or emotionally. Many men who have fairly sophisticated religious belief systems still believe that their religion gives them permission to "own" women. I don't know about all world religions, but I do know that Jesus Christ would not approve of men owning women or anyone else. That is why He spent so much time with women and why He treated them with the same respect with which He treated men. It is why He allowed Himself to be born of a woman. We're still barbaric. We just don't know it yet.

And barbarism in the name of Jesus Christ isn't just barbarism — it is pure evil.

I have two daughters. It pains me to realize that they have to be more careful where they walk than does my son. It offends me to think that, despite their obvious competence and intelligence, they may be limited in their careers simply because they were born with two X chromosomes instead of an X and a Y. I am glad that they live in 1992 and not 1892 when things were even worse for women, but that doesn't mean I must stop being offended by the sexism that still exists in our country.

After going to an all-girl prep school where she was rewarded and acknowledged for thinking and achieving, my editor, Barbara Nichols, experienced something quite different while at Marquette University. She told me she was put down for those same qualities. She was covertly encouraged to feel as if it were shameful, even a sin, to be a bright woman.

As Marcus Borg correctly pointed out, the status of women during Christ's time was even worse. Women were less than second-class citizens and were excluded from any and all religious or intellectual discourse. He stated that "a respectable Jewish man was not to talk much with women," since it was a waste of time because they were seen "as not very bright," and because they were "seductive."

And yet, as Borg and many other theologians and historians have highlighted, Jesus' behavior toward women was remarkable and "shocking." He was surrounded by both men and women. He taught women and discussed matters of faith with women, which was unheard of. He included women as equals. He was way ahead of His time. I do not believe that Jesus Christ wanted us to rest on our laurels when it came to matters of dignity and respect for women.

Men

What of men? Much has been written about us since the 1960s. Much of it is true, too. For us to have been allowed to have a place in history that includes rape, murder, violence, insensitivity and lack of feeling surely means that we have been spiritually damaged. Many of us are so frightened and so dependent upon women for our emotional well-being that we have few behavioral options outside of arrogance and violence. What kind of spirituality could a man have if he chooses to bash a woman in the teeth with a brick because she expresses her own opinion?

In my work with men's therapy groups I stress personal responsibility for both appropriate expression of emotion and appropriate means for meeting one's needs. I have empathy for how hard it is for a man to allow himself to be vulnerable and for how clumsy we first feel when we try to express more than anger or lust. I encourage men to experience their shame — shame about their emotional inadequacy, about their role in society and the family, about being offenders and about being the victims of physical and sexual abuse. The result of this is awe-inspiring and humbling. Many men are tired of being offenders or victims or both. As they take their rightful place in the world *beside* women, they become kind, powerful and truly spiritual.

Native Americans

On New Year's Day, 1992, I flew to Minot, North Dakota, for the honor of speaking at a Native American Reservation. I was met at the airport by Bob and Judy Brugh, both members of one of the tribes. We headed out onto the vast North Dakota prairie, engaged in pleasant conversation as we watched the sun set behind low-lying clouds on the horizon. I was amazed at the spirituality that still remained in members of the three tribes there —

the Mandan, the Hidatsa and the Arickara. I was amazed because the 4,000 or so people who lived on that reservation had every reason to be totally dispirited.

"What we non-Indians did to these three tribes is unforgivable," I said to myself. It hurt my spirit to see it. It made me feel ashamed.

As Bob Brugh and Jerry Irwin explained to me, we cornered the Native Americans and backed them onto a reservation where they learned again to live peacefully and in harmony with the land and with themselves. Prior to the 1950s, they had almost no alcoholism on this reservation. They had a strong Native American spirituality which they actively practiced. They had horses, a small lumber mill along the river and rich bottom land that allowed them to produce their own food in abundance. They had self-respect, purpose and dignity. Now they have high rates of alcoholism, very little food, few ways to produce income, a lot of poverty, anger, apathy and a deep abiding sadness.

What happened around 1950? We non-Indians were once again unjust and cruel. The U.S. Army Corps of Engineers decided to dam up the river to provide hydroelectric power for cities and to control the river flow. When it came to picking a spot for the dam, there were a couple of choices. One was to put it several miles upstream from the reservation so that the 4,000 Native Americans who had already been horrifyingly abused by us would not be insulted and further damaged. The other was to put the dam below the reservation thereby flooding the reservation and forcing the Native Americans to move to the high ground, away from the river bottom, where they would find no tillable soil, where there would be no trees and no lumber mill and where their new way of life since moving to the reservation would be pretty much wiped out.

You must know the rest of the story by now. Upstream from the reservation lived a couple of successful farmers who would have lost their farms had the dam been built there. On the reservation lived 4,000 Native Americans who in the 1950s had little political clout and who were probably still reeling from the victimization and abuse of the late 1800s. Of course the Corps of Engineers chose to flood the reservation. The only logic that seems to fit here is: A white farmer must be worth at least 4,000 Indians.

If this were not enough, the final blow that has kept these people's spirits suppressed and aching was the last promise that the federal government made to them and then did not keep. You and I, through our elected representatives in Congress, promised to give these people roughly $43 million, in today's dollars, all of which was to be used for capital improvements, such as a hospital, better schools and so forth. None of the money was going to go into anyone's personal pockets. The tribal elders were simply told that if they didn't accept the deal, they'd be forced off the land anyway, so of course they accepted the deal. After all, by then the federal government had the atomic bomb. What could 4,000 Native Americans do in the face of that kind of military might?

As of this writing, January 1992, these 4,000 courageous, proud, devastated, hurt, damaged, untrusting, abused, angry, disappointed and yet still spiritual Native Americans have not seen one nickel of their money. After 40 years of lobbying in Washington, D.C., they have finally managed to get a bill passed in Congress mandating the money, but at this time the Bush administration claims that there is no money in the budget for the payments to be made. It's shameful. In today's federal budget, $43 million is almost nothing.

Given our apparent lack of respect for humanity and our apparent lack of accountability for destroying the Native Americans of this hemisphere, it could be another 40 years before they see any of that money. It will never restore them to the type of lifestyle that they used to have, but it will at least allow them to begin their grieving process and move on to a workable lifestyle.

As one of the tribal elders said during the portion of my talk on abuse and depression, "We haven't grieved the loss of our land back in the 1950s. And until we grieve, we won't be able to move forward." She is right. Not only can they not grieve, they cannot forgive either because the mistake has not been corrected. So these 4,000 dignified human beings continue to suffer grief, outrage and shame because we lack the ability to be accountable for our mistakes. Yes, I felt ashamed because I am a white man. But I felt outraged because I am a human being.

What I have just told you is a true story about spiritual abuse. Why is it spiritual abuse? Because our treatment of these human beings damaged their spirits. It damaged their belief in the goodness of life. It damaged their ability to have childlike awe and wonder about the universe. It damaged their ability to have trusting relationships with others. It damaged their faith and hope.

I was grateful to have been given two tickets to the last two World Series games in 1991. But as David and I cheered the Minnesota Twins to victory, I couldn't help feeling ashamed that the team we were playing was called the Atlanta Braves. Perhaps it would have been a more ethically balanced series had our team been called the Minnesota Bigots.

Poverty

According to *U.S. News & World Report*, 11 million people starve to death each year worldwide while 34 million Americans are overweight. In 1990 the United States spent $1.6 billion on overseas food aid while we spent $236 billion eating out at restaurants. In Mozambique, 30% to 40% of the people are continually hungry, while in the U.S., 19% are on diets. There are 5.5 million American children who are regularly hungry.

The spiritual damage that happens to kids living in poverty in the inner city is immeasurable. Their dads and moms have let them down by being poor or by being poor and addicted, regardless of whose fault that is. Society has let them down by making them poorer and poorer, siphoning off money for their education and distributing it to wealthier neighborhoods and schools, denying them proper medical care and, in general, turning its back on them. I guarantee that if you put the infant son of the most prestigious, wealthy, intellectual family in America into the poverty and hopelessness of the inner city, that infant would grow up just like everyone else in the inner city. He would grow up to be angry, addictive and appropriately revengeful toward society — and he'd probably die in a gang war somewhere on a city street.

In response to the 1992 Los Angeles riots, Tom Morganthau wrote in *Newsweek*, "What we saw in the streets of Los Angeles was the new reality of poverty in America — past due bills, so to speak, of 25 years of societal and governmental neglect."

Indulging

Look at the spiritual damage that happens to a materially indulged child who grows up in a wealthy, successful, emotionally empty family that has all the external trappings of perfection but is vacant and sterile on the inside. Some of these families try to make up for the lack of intimacy by over-providing material things to their children, which is a form of double abuse. In these cases we have children who are not getting their emotional needs met. They are not having emotional contact of any real kind with their parents. They are not observing healthy intimacy between their parents. We have children who are bought off with "things" so they learn to medicate their emptiness and pain with things. Furthermore, because these children's physical needs are so thoroughly taken care of, because everything has been handed to them on silver platters, they have been robbed of the very spiritual needs to struggle and to think, question and wonder. By the time these kids are adults, they are emotionally and spiritually numb — nearly dead inside.

Emotional Neglect

Look at the spiritual abuse that happens to a little girl who grows up in a cold, lonely, empty kind of household where no one pays any attention to her. No one ever says they love her because they don't know what love is, and when they feel faint glimmers of it, they are too afraid and ashamed to tell her. She spends most of her time alone. When she accomplishes something in school, her parents simply take it for granted. When she makes friends, her parents ignore her social accomplishments, or worse, they belittle her. There are few emotional connections in her family. There is no warmth. There is a lot of loneliness. When she grows up, she will have a very hard time making emotional connections with others. She will have a hard time trusting herself or others. She will question her own accomplishments and belittle herself as her parents did. She will be afraid to question and wonder and have awe about the universe. She will be scared and lonely. Her spirit will hurt.

In an August 1992 presentation to the Knights of Columbus in New York City, Mother Teresa addressed the question of poverty. She said, "We must thank God for the beautiful way in which we sense God in the poorest of the poor." She also said, "Pray also for the people who have suffered so much, not because they are hungry for bread, but because they are hungry for love."

Angry Dad/Nice Mom

Imagine the spiritual damage that happens to children who grow up in a family where Dad is an angry, controlling tyrant who demands that everything be done his way or not at all. Mom is compliant and kind, so the kids feel as if she is some kind of an ally, when in fact she is in collusion with Dad and doesn't even know it. When Dad rages at the kids, Mom later takes them aside and explains how Dad really loves them and how he's just having a bad day. The kids feel terrified of Dad and so overly bonded with Mom that they wouldn't be able to grow up and leave home as adults if they wanted to. Well, they'll leave home physically, but they'll carry home inside of them wherever they go.

What will these kids be like? Maybe one will become compliant, like Mom. Another may become an abuser, like Dad. All of them will be at high risk for addictions. What of their ability to be spiritual? They may be able to quote the Bible chapter and verse because Dad made them memorize it perfectly so that they'd look good in public, but there's no way they'll be truly spiritual people until they heal. There will simply be too much damage.

Forced Religion

What happens to the spirit of a child who is forced to go to painfully boring church services three or four times a week and who forces himself to smile all the while in the hopes of fitting in with his parents' plans for him? We have treated adults from families like that who have ulcers, colitis, destructive marriages and sick children. Church isn't supposed to be abusive. The healthiest churches I have seen allow children to be children when they are children, rather than asking children to be adults when they are children. If you think that last sentence was confusing, just try living in a pseudo-religious family and see how confused you get!

Spiritual Abuse

Physical, emotional, intellectual and sexual abuse are about the misuse of power and the violation of trust by people or institutions who have power over us. All abuse is spiritual abuse because it damages the spirits of those who are abused. Linda and I encounter spiritually damaged people in our psychology practices all the time and we see how it gets in their way. People who are struggling with addictions to alcohol or drugs angrily refuse to go to Alcoholics Anonymous because of "that God stuff" they talk about in AA. Their spiritual damage keeps them from trusting or surrendering to anything but their addiction. True, some AA groups misapply the Higher Power concept, but to stop acting out an addiction requires some kind of surrender. It doesn't have to be AA. Spiritually damaged people aren't about to surrender because surrender just means getting hurt by someone again.

Spirituality and surrender also affect our ability to learn from those who are stronger and wiser than we are. To be able to learn from someone who is stronger, we need to have had experiences with strength that were nonabusive. If our parents abuse or neglect us, we have been hurt by them. We also have learned that strong people, people in authority, are not to be trusted. Once that trust is violated, our spirituality also has been violated. You can see it in the employee who is always butting heads with managers at work or who is always criticizing his boss and blaming all of his problems on his boss. True, some bosses would be better off fired, but for someone who has been abused as a child, it seems that no matter where they work or how many bosses they have their problems are always the boss's fault. The boss is always evil.

Is The World All Bad?

Linda and I work with people's pain every day, and yet I am pretty certain that most of the time we feel very good about the state of humanity. I operate from the premise that we're all imperfect, that all human beings would like to treat themselves and others more respectfully, and that the more we hurt, the more likely we are to improve. My pain and my clients' pain don't scare me like they used to.

I see many Christians who learned somewhere that the more pain they can create for themselves and others, the more holy they will become. This is a very distorted interpretation of Christ's message about suffering. Yes, suffering is part of being human, spiritual and Christ-like. But to create suffering for oneself and others by being abusive or disrespectful is certainly not Christ-like. Enjoying my suffering instead of suffering in a new way so I can stop abusing myself and others is not Christ-like.

It is Christ-like to face the pain of growing up, to face the fear of getting close to other human spirits, to face the shame of admitting and changing one's flaws, to share one's painful feelings with others, to let go of our children so they can grow up and have their own lives instead of getting stuck in our lives, to let go of our addictions, to be alone at times, to right the wrongs that we have caused and to become whole. These are Christ-like pains. These are worth it.

CHAPTER 5

If Jesus Christ Had Wanted Us To Think, He Would Have Spoken To Us In Parables

Therefore I speak to them in parables, because seeing they do not see, and hearing they do not hear, nor do they understand.
Matthew 13:13

Our son, David, was involved in confirmation classes a few years ago. He and the other 14-year-olds in his class were learning about the Old and New Testaments, the principles and beliefs of the church to which we belong, the history of Christianity and many other things deemed appropriate by the talented staff who were conducting the classes. One evening it was our turn to bring the meal for these young people. We watched in wonder and nostalgia as they bantered with each other, teased, talked, kidded around and just acted like a bunch of normal teenagers. We could see that it was both fun and a struggle for these kids to be 14 and to be in confirmation class.

One evening I drove to the church to pick up David. He jumped into the car and I asked him how his class had been. He wrinkled his brow into a distinct frown, fell silent for a few moments, then blurted out with some nervousness and hesitation, "I don't know. I . . . I . . . What do you think? What do you think about all of this stuff?" Before I could ask him what he meant, he continued, "I don't know if I believe that there's a God. I don't know if I believe any of this stuff that we're learning." He was obviously struggling with some very big questions, and he seemed to be a little nervous about how I was going to react to his disclosure. There was a bit of tension in the air.

I said, "Dave, I think I understand your questioning. That's what you're supposed to be doing at your age. It's good to question what people tell you. You need to form your own conclusions about all of this some day." David seemed to like that answer. He seemed to feel safe with it. As a result of that safety we went on and had a good, challenging discussion about Christianity, atheism, belief systems and alternate explanations for creation. Indeed, it was exactly what he needed to be doing right then in his life. Had he not been doing that kind of questioning, I would have been very concerned.

As a postscript to that story I should add that recently we had been out of town a couple of weeks in a row. The next Saturday David asked, "Are we going to church tomorrow? I really miss it." I wonder if he would have said this had I shamed and criticized his attempts to think just a few short years earlier.

FOUR-YEAR-OLD MORALITY IN A FORTY-YEAR-OLD BODY: HOW KIDS LEARN

The late Jean Piaget revolutionized our understanding of cognitive development in children and adults. His work, which began when he was a boy growing up in Switzerland, is considered to be the most important work on intellectual development in this century. What Piaget did was to systematically study, document and then organize the inner world of the child's mind. For the first time in history it was possible to see and feel what it was like for a child to try to make sense out of the world around him. What Piaget discovered has been fascinating scientists and laymen alike since his earliest publications.

His theory of cognitive development states that the human mind is "wired" to adapt to the environment for survival of the individual and of the species. The way that the mind adapts is similar to the way that the body adapts. We either assimilate or accommodate to new information.

1. *ASSIMILATION:* Our minds modify what they take in to fit their preconceived notions about the world better.
2. *ACCOMMODATION:* Our minds actually modify themselves to fit new information about the world better.

When we modify what we take in to fit our current cognitive structures better, Piaget called it *assimilation*. When we modify how we view the world to fit new information better, Piaget called it *accommodation*. These two mental processes, assimilation and accommodation, are thought to be going on all the time, but one or the other will be more dominant in any given mental activity.

Let's say that an 18-month-old child has a concept of "doggie." To her, a doggie is anything that has four legs and fur. She is riding in the car with her mother and she spies a cow chomping on some grass by the roadside. She smiles and her eyes light up in a flash of recognition. "Doggie!" she exclaims to her mother.

Well, it isn't a dog. Wanting her daughter to understand the world as it truly is, her mother says gently, "No, honey, that's not a dog. That's a cow. It walks, and it has four legs and fur, but it's a different kind of animal. It doesn't eat dog food, for one thing. It's larger than our dog. In fact, the milk we have in the refrigerator comes from cows." The little girl looks at her mother, looks at the cow, looks puzzled, stares off into space for a moment as the wheels of her mind turn furiously — and then she shouts excitedly, "DOGGIE!" It's too much for her to handle at this tender age, so she assimilates the cow into her existing mental structures. She makes the cow fit into her notion of "doggie."

Is our little girl dumb? Is there something wrong with her brain? Certainly not. She is making sense out of her world the way she is supposed to for her age. As she encounters more cows and more walking things that aren't dogs, she will eventually accommodate to the reality outside of her. Eventually she will change her existing mental structures to fit the world better. In other words, her mind will become more complex and better organized. It will include the notion of "walking things" that has subcategories of "dog," "cat," "cow," "sheep," "lion" and so on.

One of Piaget's greatest accomplishments was to show us that the thinking of a four-year-old is qualitatively different from the thinking of an eight-year-old, and that the thinking of an eight-year-old is qualitatively different from that of an eighteen-year-old. This means a four-year-old is not dumber than an eight-year-old. The four-year-old simply lives in a different reality than the eight-year-old. The four-year-old constructs a different universe. If you are following all of this, you will see that your own understanding of the world goes in stages. From birth to age two you view the world one way. From two to seven you view it in a new way. From seven to eleven you view it in yet another way.

Let's look at another example. Suppose I take two equal lumps of clay, show them to you and let you prove by weighing them that they're equal. If I rolled them up into two equal-sized balls, you'd say they were equal, right? Then if I flattened one of the balls into a sausage shape and asked you if the two chunks of clay still had the same amount, you would say yes. If you perform this little experiment in front of a typical four-year-old, he will say that either the sausage or the ball shape now has more clay in it even though it doesn't. Is our four-year-old dumb? Is there something wrong with his brain? No. He's just viewing the world the way that a four-year-old does. He's being normal.

If this seems pretty elementary, let's move up the age/intelligence scale a long way to an understanding of time and space as Albert Einstein understood them. To most of us, time and space are independent of each other. To Einstein, they were not. Does this mean that our reality is invalid and that we are hopelessly retarded and incapable of functioning on this earth? No. It just means that we still have things to learn and we don't know it all. It's fair to say that when you know it all, you're God.

Time, space, weak nuclear force, unified field theory, quarks, black holes, you name it. There are many things which are beyond the comprehension of the average person and which are still true. At some point we simply have to take it on faith that reality as "the experts" see it is true. We make this leap of faith every time we use a telephone or watch something on television.

Through his brilliant work Piaget taught us that at each stage of human development we need to be challenged by the thinking of the next higher stage. In the example of the clay being rolled out into a sausage shape, the child needs to experience gradually through hands-on example that the amount of clay remains the same even if you change the shape. Here is the critical piece of this challenging notion: If we challenge a child's thinking with concepts that are more than one stage ahead of where he is, the child will become overwhelmed, shut down and get stuck in immature thinking indefinitely. If I throw concepts of Einstein's theory of relativity at a four-year-old, he'll get overwhelmed, shut down and not want to think anymore at all.

Piaget's impressive work also shows us that children and adults learn through hands-on experience first. This means that if you want your child to grasp the reality of "Love thy neighbor as thyself," the worst way to do it is to make him memorize it, spout the words at him all the time, abuse him emotionally with it, then go out yourself and treat other human beings abusively. His hands-on experience will tell the child that this love thy neighbor stuff is crazy.

The best way to teach a child the value of "love thy neighbor as thyself" is to treat yourself, your family, your children, your friends, Native Americans, Jews, Catholics, Muslims, Hindus, Protestants, Caucasians, African-Americans, Hispanic-Americans, Asian-Americans, you-name-it, with the respect, dignity and value due any human being. If we do this, our children will experience the feelings of warmth, love, tolerance and respect. Then when it comes time for them to deal with the abstract concept of love, they will know what it means because they have experienced it day after day as they watched you. In other words, if you want to raise healthy, spiritual children:

1. Challenge children, but not beyond their capabilities.
2. Live it, don't preach it.

The Challenge Of Separation

When children become teenagers, it suddenly becomes their life risk to challenge much of what they have been told during childhood. This questioning and searching that makes up so much of adolescence is crucial to their later success and emotional adjustment as adults. Jesus Christ knew this, Erik Erikson knew this, Jean Piaget knew this, Jane Loevinger knew this — and in my heart-of-hearts I believe every parent knows this, too. I just know that deep down inside, even the most abusive, controlling parent knows this questioning is part of being a clear, whole, healthy human being. Parents may fear it because they haven't done it themselves or because it means their children will grow up, but I believe they somehow know it.

If you're having a hard time understanding this period in your teen's development, think back to when he or she was two years old. Do you remember the "terrible twos?" They weren't all that terrible. They were exciting. They were the "exciting twos" because your children stated clearly for the first time that they were separate from you. They said the word "no!" They ran away from you. They got into things in ways you never imagined, which explains why the term "childproof" is a metaphysical impossibility. They were saying to you, to me and to the world, "I am me! I am not you! I am separate!" The "terrible twos" are so marvelous because they offer a subtle hint of the ultimate goal held by both parents and children in a healthy family — inevitable separation.

I remember my daughter Kristin tugging on the refrigerator door one hot summer day when she was about two-and-a-half. I was a typical new parent who over-anticipated my first child's every need. I asked in a rather solicitous, fawning tone, "Would you like something to drink, Kristin?" She quickly shot back, "No!" "Okay, dear," I replied. I stood there and watched her struggle with that refrigerator door for what seemed like an eternity until it suddenly swung open. At that instant the heavens opened up and allowed me to witness one of the simple miracles of creation. It was the absolutely satisfied, ecstatic look of accomplishment that swept across Kristin's face as she opened the door by herself. "Oh," I thought, "She's supposed to be doing things on her own now."

I remember trying to use behavior modification to teach something to my daughter Rebecca while the video cameras were rolling. I had hoped to use the tape in one of my graduate seminars as a demonstration of how to use behavioral principles with very young children. As would happen with a bumbling college professor, I wasn't fully prepared as the cameras began. I sat in front of Rebecca with a bowl of ice on a hot summer day and told her to say "Mommy!" Knowing that her Mommy was not a bowl of ice chips, Rebecca cried out, plaintively, because she was hot and thirsty, "Ice!" I withdrew the bowl of ice and said, "Say Mommy!" Rebecca looked at me, looked down below her highchair where I had stashed the bowl of ice and cried out louder, "Ice!"

I was determined to have Rebecca say "Mommy" on command, and Rebecca was determined to get her ice come hell or high water. Back and forth we went as the camera rolled. It is to Rebecca's credit that she did not give up demanding her ice for a long time. Yes, she eventually said "Mommy!" when I told her to "Say Mommy!" And yes, for that one brief, eternal moment I was again treated by the heavens to that most rare of celestial events — a child's face lighting up with the excitement and pride of having accomplished something difficult, despite her father's ineptitude.

From those exciting first stirrings of separateness in our children when they are two years old, through early childhood, elementary school and then junior high school, healthy parents get more and more excited about their children's independence of thought and action. At the same time, unhealthy, unspiritual parents get more and more frightened of their children's thinking and independence. The thought of being without dependent children is too much for some parents. Fear of abandonment is what usually breeds totalitarianism, and that's what happens in families where Dad and Mom haven't grown up themselves.

Little Ralph: What Happens When Kids Don't Get To Think?

If kids learn from what we do, and if they can only become mental adults if we nurture their minds in the right ways, at the right rate and in ways that are healthy and whole, then what happens when kids aren't encouraged to separate and grow up? How do they get stuck and what are they like later?

Ralph grew up in what appeared to be a warm, loving family. His parents were active in the community, volunteering to help the poor and helping out with hospital fund drives. They had respectable jobs as a teacher and a nurse. They participated in most of the activities at their Christian church. In fact, as a family they were admired by the majority of the folks in their community. They were model citizens, model friends, model parents, model partners and model Christians. They prided themselves in being deeply devoted to their religion and their religious beliefs, and they sorely desired to have their children be equally religious and committed to their religious beliefs.

From the time little Ralph was 18 months old, his parents began to teach him about the life of Jesus Christ, about Christ's suffering, about the Father, the Son and the Holy Spirit, and about all the other mysteries of Christianity. They loved to talk about all of these things with Ralph, and Ralph seemed to love to talk to them, too. When Ralph was five years old, they sent him to Sunday school where he learned even more about Christianity. Being five, though, meant that a lot of what they were trying to teach him went right over his head. He simply assimilated all that he learned into what he already knew about the world. As much as they tried to get him to understand the spiritual mysteries of their religion, all little Ralph could do was think of God as a man with a beard who sits on the clouds and watches us and rewards or punishes us. This is all most five-year-olds can conceptualize about God.

As Ralph grew older, he took in more and more of what they taught him. But it seemed that the more he took in, the less it meant to him in any personal way. In fact, what he discovered later was that he only believed what they were telling him because he wanted to be a good child and to be loved by his parents. He was eventually too caught up in this "parent-pleasing" to ever let on that he didn't understand what his parents were telling him or, even worse, that he wasn't always sure if he believed it. He went all the way through childhood looking like the perfect little Christian, making his parents' dream come true and making his parents look even more wonderful in public than they already did.

Something else happened, too. In their zeal to be good Christians and to have little Ralph be one, too, they did some things that weren't good at all. Ralph's parents had some big problems with sexuality, for example, which left them feeling a lot of embarrassment and shame about sex. Instead of working this shame through, they disguised it within their religious system and made it seem as if it was part of Christianity to be afraid of and disgusted with sex. They unconsciously passed this belief on to Ralph just by being around him during his childhood.

Somewhere they also got the distorted idea that good Christians never get angry or raise their voices. They believed good Christians work themselves to death taking care of everyone else in the community first, even if it means neglecting their own children, spouses and marriages. Little Ralph also learned that to be a good Christian one must never get angry and one must always give of oneself first, until there's no self left. In other words, little Ralph learned to be terribly self-neglectful because his parents had been terribly neglectful and didn't even know it.

What happened through all of this is that Ralph became spiritually numb and spiritually stuck very early in life. He heard people say "love your neighbor as yourself," but what he saw people do was neglect themselves and get burned out for the sake of looking perfect. He saw people fail to grow up into mature spiritual beings. His parents had the morality of four-year-olds in adult bodies, so that's what he learned. He never learned to question or use the marvelous powers of his God-given brain to search for the Truth in a way that would be personally meaningful for him. He couldn't admit it publicly as an adult, but in his heart-of-hearts Ralph still thought of God as a man with a beard who sits on the clouds. This God dispensed rewards and punishments. He occasionally went into a blind rage and punished everybody for the mistakes of a few because this is what Ralph's father did.

The *coup de grace* in all of Ralph's troubles was that in his desperate search for real love and acceptance, and because of the sexual shame that he learned from his parents, Ralph was terrified of relationships, especially with women. He was among the many men who feared and hated women.

What better profession could there be for such a man than the ministry? He had been trained and encouraged since early childhood. He was gently seductive in such an ever-so-nice way. He never expressed his anger directly, which endeared him to all of those in his flock who were powerless and waiting to be seduced. He could quote the Bible backwards or forwards, and do it in his sleep. He'd never thought about or questioned any of it. To many people he seemed like a safe haven in a dangerous world. Ralph was ready for a stint in the ministry.

By the time he went to inpatient treatment for his sexual acting-out with all the women in his flock, Little Ralph was ready to start growing up. But what a painful way to learn and become spiritual.

IF JESUS HAD WANTED US TO THINK, HE WOULD HAVE SPOKEN TO US IN PARABLES

The simple truth is that we learn by example. We learn to love one another if we see our parents love each other and us. We learn to take care of ourselves if we see our parents take care of themselves and us. We learn compassion, humility, dignity, wisdom and grace if we see adults around us model those feelings and behaviors. We also learn to think, question, wonder, separate and grow up — if our parents have done the same in their own lives. No one knew this better than Jesus Christ.

He wanted us to think. Much of His teaching was in metaphors and parables. He has left us to struggle with their meanings ever since. As Mortimer Adler noted, One thing should be pointed out about the Golden Rule and that is "its vacuity as a precept of conduct unless it is filled in with an understanding of what is really good for any human being and, in consequence, an understanding of what is right for all others."

We are supposed to struggle and think. That is the essence of the human drama. In totalitarian systems throughout history, people's minds are manipulated with simple, pat answers that play to our fear of survival and our hatreds. Black-and-white thinking is how a child thinks. Tell a child that all men are evil and it makes life much less complicated. "I don't have to deal with men at all," she says to herself. "Mommy taught me that all men are bad." See? When it's this simple, she dosen't have to think anymore. She simply fears and hates instead.

Maturity, holiness and true Christianity require much more than pat answers which play on fear and hatred. Jesus' method of teaching — by His example and by metaphors and parables — makes that very clear to me. It is more difficult to think than simply to have pat answers. But it is also the road to a mature spirituality and relationship with God.

CHAPTER 6

Daddy, What's A Myth?

No one, when he has lit a lamp, covers it with a vessel or puts it under a bed, but sets it on a lampstand, that those who enter may see the light.

Luke 8:16

This is a revised version of a story I first wrote in 1979. So that you don't interpret it in a way that was not intended, I will commit the ultimate writer's sin and tell you what this story is about instead of letting you interpret it as you wish. I don't have the confidence in my teaching ability that Christ had in His. It is not about Christianity being a myth. I am a Christian and I do not believe that Christianity is a myth. It is simply a story about the beautiful things that happen between people when they question and wonder together.

Once upon a time there were two little girls and a little boy, sisters and brother. One day they were talking about something, arguing actually. As they often did, they went to their father. All three of them chimed in, "Daddy, what's a myth?" Like most fathers, Dad was proud to have them think he was so smart. Instead of giving them a quick answer, he paused and thought for a moment, which was good, because it gave the children time to think, too.

Kristin, who was the oldest, jumped in first. "I just learned about myths in school. Our teacher said they were stories that people made up a long time ago to explain things like the weather and the stars because they didn't know as much about the world as we do now."

"You catch on fast, Kristin," said Dad, wondering what Rebecca and David were about to say. They were younger, but they could think, too.

"Yeah, Dad," Rebecca piped in. "I said a myth is just a story and Kristin said it was only one kind of story. It's a story, isn't it?"

Then David, the youngest, joined the discussion. "It's a story about how the world works. Maybe it is just one kind of story. I don't know."

Dad was trying to keep it all straight. "Well, you're all right. It's a story, it's a special kind of story, and it can be used to explain how the world works, among other things."

The kids were getting confused.

Dad had to think fast. "But there are probably other definitions of 'myth' that we don't even know. Maybe some that we don't understand. Why don't we go look in the dictionary and see?" So they did.

Dad said, "I'll read them off and each of you can write one of them down. Then we can look at them one by one."

When they were done, there was one definition that they all seemed to be looking at. It read, "Any fictitious or imaginary story, person or thing."

"What does that mean?" David asked.

"Dave, it's like a made-up story about something. You know, like Paul Bunyan," Rebecca offered.

"Yeah," Kristin said. "It means something made up. Something make-believe. So it's more than just a story to explain the weather. It could be a made-up story about anything."

"Close enough," Dad said. He was so pleased with their enthusiastic thinking that he wasn't about to nitpick.

"But we're still not clear," shouted the kids.

"I know," Dad replied. He cared a lot about the three of them and he really wanted them to understand. "What if I told you that there was a 5,000-pound green giraffe in town who sneaks around at night and trims the branches off of all the tall trees? That would be a myth."

"I get it. A myth is a giraffe," the kids squealed in unison.

"Would that really be a myth?" asked Dad. "I mean, do you really know for sure that there truly isn't a big green giraffe like that?"

"Oh, c'mon, Dad, you're really being silly," David said.

"Yeah, Dad. Be serious," added Rebecca.

"What's your point?" asked Kristin.

The kids looked at each other and giggled and grinned and laughed and kidded. Dad laughed, too. They were having a wonderful time being silly, even if they weren't quite solving the mystery of a myth at the moment.

And then the three kids said, "Who cares? A myth is a big green giraffe who trims trees!" Then they laughed and giggled some more. They were getting bored.

They hadn't come up with any final answers, but they'd had fun and learned something, too. So Dad said, "Let's go down to the beach and go swimming. It's getting hot."

"Goodie!" shouted the kids. "Last one in is a rotten egg!"

So they went swimming.

A few days later when the kids were walking with their father, Kristin said, "Dad, do you know what I learned in school today?"

"No. What did you learn in school today?"

"Guess, Dad. You have to guess first," she pleaded.

Sometimes he liked to guess, but he'd been working all morning and he wasn't in the mood. "I can't guess. I'm all guessed-out."

Kristin cheerfully continued, "Oh, all right, Dad. I learned that George Washington's real birthday is on the same day as Rebecca's."

"That's true," Dad said. "What else did you learn?" The kids were starting to get interested again.

"I also learned that when he was a little boy he chopped down a cherry tree and when his father asked him who did it, he said, 'I cannot tell a lie. I chopped down the cherry tree.' That's because he was a very honest person, and he became the first President of the United States," she added proudly.

"I learned that in school, too," Rebecca said.

"I did, too," said David.

Dad looked thoughtful. "That's a nice story, kids. I learned that one in school, too. But do you know what?" He wasn't sure if he should continue or not. It was sort of like being asked if there really was a Santa Claus.

"What?" they all asked with deepening interest. Now he had to go on.

"When I was older and learned more about George Washington and America, I found out that he didn't chop down a cherry tree at all."

"Oh, no, Dad, that's not true," the three kids asserted. They thought Dad was teasing them again.

"Yes, it is," Dad said. "When we get home, I'll show you a book that tells about it."

The kids were confused and excited. When they got home, Dad found a book, *History Of The George Washington Bicentennial Celebration*. It said the story of George Washington and the cherry tree ". . . was originated by the Reverend Mason Locke Weems . . . No evidence to prove this story has been found. In writing this work, Weems gave full play to his imagination without very much regard for historical facts, even acknowledging that he did this for moral purposes."

"Gee," the kids frowned. "Our teachers lied to us about that."

"Did they?" Dad asked. "Maybe not. Maybe they didn't do it on purpose. Do you remember when we were talking about myths?"

"Oh, sure, Dad. That was fun. The big green giraffe."

"Right," said Dad. "Is this story about George Washington a lie or a myth?"

"Hmmm," Kristin said thoughtfully.

"I don't know," said Rebecca. "Is a myth a lie?"

"Yeah, what's the story here?" asked David.

"Let me think," Dad began slowly, wanting to be quite clear. "Sometimes we pretend something is true because it's fun to believe it. So we all agree that we believe it even though we know that it isn't exactly true."

"What are you trying to say, Dad?" they asked.

"I'm not sure that I can explain it very well to you, but let's take our giraffe story. We all know people go around in trucks and trim the trees, right?"

"Right, Dad."

"But what if everyone in our town decided to say that a big green giraffe did it at night when we were all asleep? Wouldn't that be fun? I mean, pretty soon everyone would be talking about the big green giraffe. They'd be laughing and smiling and winking at each other. It would be their big secret. One they could all share."

"We get it, Dad."

"Would we be lying?" Dad asked.

"Well, not really," the kids admitted. "We'd know that it wasn't really true, and who would be hurt?"

"Probably no one," Dad said. "Just like it's fun to believe that George Washington cut down the cherry tree when he was a little boy."

"Now we see!" The kids were relieved. "Our teachers weren't lying to us. They were telling us a myth. Even if they didn't know the real story behind it, they were still just telling us a myth."

Impish grins swept across their faces. "Let's ask them and see if they know the real story!"

"Yes," Dad said. "Go ahead and ask. It won't hurt to ask."

After Dad got home from work the next day, the excited kids bounded into the house. "Guess what, Dad! None of our teachers knew the real story about George Washington and the cherry tree. They didn't know it was a myth. Can you believe it? They thought that story was true!"

"What do you make of it?" Dad asked, holding his breath, waiting for their answers.

"We guess it shows that sometimes it's hard to tell the difference between what's real and what isn't," they all said together.

Dad sat quietly, proud of his three children, but also wondering what it all meant for him. "You know, it makes me wonder if people ever tell lies. They might just all be special myths that everyone believes in all by themselves. You know, like what people used to believe about the sun and the moon and the stars."

"Uh, Dad . . ." the kids said cautiously. "Let's not get onto another heavy topic right away. We've been thinking hard about all of this stuff for several days."

"You're right," he agreed. This time he was tired of thinking, too. "Let's go swimming!" he shouted.

"Last one in is a rotten egg!" the kids yelled. The four of them ran down toward the lake, enjoying the warm air and the lazy afternoon. "Last one in is a rotten egg!"

CHAPTER 7

Beliefs, Re-enactments And "The Vow"

Let the little children come to Me, and do not forbid them; for of such is the kingdom of God.

Luke 18:16

THE IMPORTANCE OF OUR BELIEFS

What we believe about the world and about each other is very important. Our beliefs can determine how we live our lives and how we feel about the world. To give a simple example, many little children believe that on December 24, a magic person somehow flies all around the planet and leaves toys for all of the world's children. If you were to tell these children that Santa Claus didn't exist, they would either laugh in disbelief, get angry at your teasing or be hurt and scared by the possibility of truth in your statement.

Some people believe in "the little people," whether they be gnomes, elves, leprechauns or Hawaiian menehunes.

These little people can be used to explain all sorts of things from magic to mischief. Because of his short stature and thick, protruding brow, early anthropologists believed Neanderthal Man was not very intelligent. This is why we refer to some brutish, domineering, uncouth men today as "Neanderthals." Some anthropologists are beginning to reconsider this interpretation of the fossil record. Maybe some day Neanderthals will have their good name and reputation restored, and we will have to come up with a new term for brutish men.

Some humans believe that women are better than men or that men are better than women. This belief has caused centuries of misery for both sexes because when you believe that one sex is better, you wind up treating the people of the other sex as if they were not human. We now know that this treatment causes both parties to be unhappy at the very least, and that it can lead to horrendous physical and emotional abuse at its worst.

According to a 1991 Gallup Poll cited in *U.S. News & World Report*, 47% of all Americans believe "God created man pretty much in his present form at one time within the last 10,000 years." Forty percent believe that God created everything in the universe but that this happened over millions of years and included man's evolution from other species. Nine percent believe that everything evolved on its own, without any Supreme Being involved.

There are probably people somewhere on the planet who still believe that the world is flat and that, if you walk too far in a straight line, you'll fall off the edge of the earth into oblivion. What we believe about the world is very important. It will determine certain things we want to do and don't want to do. If I believed that the world was flat, I'd be very careful about walking long distances in a straight line, especially in the dark.

Differing Christian Beliefs

There are many branches of Christianity and, along with them, many systems of belief. Those of us who were raised in a Christian tradition learned at least some of these. Most Christians believe that Jesus Christ was both Man and God, that His life on earth and subsequent Resurrection are what allow us to be forgiven and redeemed. Most people who call themselves Christians believe in the Father, the Son and the Holy Spirit, although not all do. These are broad beliefs that are a matter of faith. They have become doctrine in most Christian churches. Everyone in that particular church usually believes the same thing about these broad doctrines.

The more specific we get about our Christian beliefs, the more disagreement there seems to be among the various Christian religions. This is why there are still so many different branches of Christianity. As Huston Smith noted in his book on comparative religion entitled *The Religions Of Man*, Jesus was not always crystal clear about what He was saying that we should do. Smith noted:

> Jesus' teachings contain no simple rule of thumb as to what overt acts are required of us. To be a follower of Christ is not to be relieved of the responsibility to think.

Jesus definitely left us plenty of room to think about what He said. He spoke in parables much of the time and parables are open to various interpretations. This is one reason why theologians and church leaders have debated the various nuances of meaning in what Christ said ever since His death. Because of this, many human beings since Christ's time have come up with sometimes frightening interpretations of what His life meant. Some people beat their children, even kill them and justify it in the name of Jesus. Others hate themselves and live in a dark pool of fear and shame most of their lives. A thoughtful man or woman might ask, "How can this happen?"

RE-ENACTMENTS AND "THE VOW"

Southern Baptist minister and educator Myron C. Madden wrote a small and powerful book in 1970, entitled *The Power To Bless.* This book was given to me by two friends and colleagues, Joe Baroody and John Schumacher, who are Baptist ministers working in South Carolina. In his book, Reverend Madden has carefully integrated centuries of Christian thinking with what we now know about child and adult psychology in a way that I can only call marvelously healing. It is a gentle book that asks the reader to examine and ultimately strengthen his or her Christian beliefs.

One of the concepts Madden discussed within the framework of Christianity is very similar to the concept of reenactment that is part of modern family systems theory. Linda and I use this concept a lot in working with survivors of painful families. Madden's term for it is *The Vow.*

The Vow is a stance toward life or a set of underlying, covert beliefs that we generate in childhood as a result of what happens to us then. Upon reaching adulthood, we carry this hidden Vow with us and try to play it out as best we can, even though we are most likely not even aware of it.

This concept and its more clinical name, re-enactment, helps us to understand some of the most puzzling and painful things that we Christians do despite our faith. Long before the Adult Children of Alcoholics movement, Reverend Madden wrote: "The man who denies his childhood is not rid of it," and "A man will often go against reason simply because the child within has first call on his energies. This is especially true of the man who has little insight into his 'child of the past.' "

Whether we know it or not, each of us has a set of beliefs inside of us that determine how we think, feel and act. To complicate matters, we have two sets of beliefs.

One set of beliefs is *overt* — the ones that we profess publicly, such as "a good Christian loves all people." The other set of beliefs is *covert* — ones based on the Vows we made as children. These often contradict the overt beliefs. If one's mother leaned on her son for emotional support when he was a child, which is unconsciously very frightening and abusive to a child, he might unconsciously believe that "women are dangerous and must be controlled and punished harshly to keep them at bay." This belief, of course, is directly at odds with his professed belief that a good Christian loves all people.

A Damaging Vow In Detail

We humans are vulnerable and imperfect. Each one of us has our breaking point. Suppose that I grow up in a violent family with a lot of yelling and screaming. As a little child I will be fearful of this. I will worry that Daddy and Mommy might hurt each other or me. I will lie in my bed at night and listen to the fighting with knots in my stomach and fear in my breathing passages. As I endure this throughout my childhood, I will begin to form my Vow back in the recesses of my mind. My Vow is quite straightforward — when I grow up, I will not have violence in my relationships. It is a noble, honorable and initially sad statement that we all make about one part of our childhoods or another. It is sad because, according to the Principle of Re-enactment, we are destined to reenact our childhood pain until we have identified it and healed from it.

Unfortunately, because my Vow was made with the understanding and insight of a little child, I will carry into adulthood this same understanding. To heal my childhood means to face back into it, which is too painful at first. For example, as a young married man I might create a family system in which anger is feared and therefore not allowed. I may have married a young woman with a similar Vow, so together we create a family with "no anger." Tragically, there is no such thing as a family with no anger because anger is a healthy feeling that all people feel when they are intruded upon in large or small ways. There is anger in a "no-anger family." Because of our reenactment it just spills out sideways and hurts everyone even worse than if it were direct. This is what we call being passive-aggressive.

After a while I am so unaware of what is making me angry that I simply begin to resent my wife in general terms. I get annoyed when she walks into the room. I get angry when she makes a mistake. I pick on her for the littlest things. I use sarcasm and teasing and cruel jokes and humor to hurt her. When she says "Stop," I claim innocence by saying, "I didn't mean any harm by it. Can't you tell I was just kidding?" Or worse, I accuse her of having the problem. "You're so sensitive, so touchy. You always were a touchy person."

After a few months or years of this, one or the other of us explodes in a rage of pent-up anger, and then we really let each other have it. Or, if we're still controlling all that anger, we will become seriously depressed or develop lots of physical symptoms and illnesses such as chronic headaches, ulcers, colitis and high blood pressure.

The Religion Double Bind

Now let's add a religious element to the equation. Remember that I am afraid of anger. It would help me to hang onto the fear if I could somehow tie it into a meaning system that at least implied that anger was bad. I find myself drawn to the healing words and teachings of Jesus Christ. I join a little congregation down the street when I'm still a teenager. My parents think it's funny. I find comfort and solace in the church despite my parents' amusement.

There's only one drawback. Everyone who belongs to the church seems to have problems with anger. Many of them have ulcers or colitis or headaches. They all have saintly smiles on their faces even though they are grinding their teeth in anger and wheezing in fear. But it all seems "normal" to me because that's consistent with the Vow that I made earlier in my childhood.

I learn all about the Bible but my Vow only lets me hear what I want to hear and see what I want to see. I am wandering in the darkness, groping for answers. I have a distorted belief that Jesus Christ did not express anger, which is reinforcing my Vow not to be angry. As a young married man, I find that it is killing me as well as my wife, but I don't know what to do or where to go.

This sets up an incredibly painful double bind. If I express my anger directly, I believe that I will be as awful and hurtful as my parents were to me. It will also mean that I am a "bad" Christian. If I don't express my anger directly, I will hurt myself and others with my passive-aggressive anger. I will also get sick or remain sick. This is such a terrible trap that eventually I will do the unthinkable — I will rage uncontrollably and become just like the rageful parents I have been trying to be unlike for the past 25 or 35 years.

Linda and I work with this type of double-binding re-enactment in almost every case we treat. It is extremely common. Somewhere in childhood we promise to do it differently but nobody taught us how. Then, when it turns out to be a distorted or misguided promise, we stick with it anyway because it is all we have to hang on to. Inside we know that what we are doing is hurting us and others. We don't know what to do and we have nowhere to turn, so we just keep hanging on to the pain out of self-protection.

The saddest part of this double bind is that Jesus Christ *did* tell us how to get out of it. We need to admit our mistake, ask for help from another, correct the mistake and ask for forgiveness. It is an incredibly powerful act to admit one's weaknesses and to ask for help and acceptance. When we are almost completely lost and in pain, it is time to admit that we can't do it alone. It is our fear and our inner pain that keep us rigidly holding onto a lifestyle or belief that causes damage. When we are stuck, we need to admit it to people who are safe and who have the wisdom to help. Surrendering to a con artist or an offender is dangerous. Surrendering to someone who has our best interests at heart is the way to heal. Finding people who can help us but not use us is the key.

Other Destructive Re-enactments

So you can see how one's past can unconsciously interfere with a richer, deeper practice of Christianity. I would like to offer two more examples of how the Vow can get in our way.

The Happy One

Perhaps your father or mother was sick or depressed during most of your childhood. As a result you carried a great deal of pity and sadness for them. In the depths of his depression Dad would share with you how bad he felt and how hopeless the world seemed. Unable to cope with Dad's illness by herself, and unwilling to take the risk to talk with other adults outside of the family, Mom began to rely on you for support.

The two adults on whom you are supposed to be able to rely are relying on you. Childhood is no longer safe. You muster all the energy you can to keep the household happy and upbeat. You become the energy that drives the family. You are the only thing that can pull Dad and Mom out of the doldrums. You become a thing. An object. Alienated. You become a live-in energizer and antidepressant for the family.

Early on you make a promise to yourself which you believe will prevent this kind of trouble in your own life when you grow up. You vow never to be depressed and not to focus on the sad things in life. This becomes a re-enactment of the childhood neglect you experienced with Dad and Mom because the core trauma you endured as a child was to be unable to be vulnerable. By vowing not to have your sadness, you prevent yourself from ever healing the childhood wounds that you carried into adulthood. As a result you will almost inevitably become emotionally blunted and shut down. You may find yourself driven to engage in constant, frenetic activity to keep the feelings away and therefore "to keep the blues away." You may talk and think incessantly, work obsessively, all to ensure that you never experience the depression which plagued your father.

The more you deny your sadness, which is not the same thing as depression, the more you will push yourself toward the very depression you are avoiding. You create an even more painful double bind if you then reinforce this painful approach to life with the distorted Christian belief that you should always be joyful no matter what — which is not what Christ did at all.

The solution to this bind is to find somewhere you can safely be vulnerable when you need to be. The powerful shields that you had to put up to be "the strong one" for Dad and Mom must come down. You must be the one to take them down; no one should try to make you take them down until it is safe. At the same time, you are the only one who can seek out that safety. So you must risk with wisdom. You must keep searching, get hurt, nurture your wounds, make mistakes and learn from them. You must have faith. Jesus said that we must seek. Rely on your faith in Him but remember that He was clear about this: Love and spirituality and holiness come not just from faith in Him, but from each other. He said we need to be with each other while on earth. Just praying isn't enough. We need to pray and seek out each other.

The Perfect One

Linda and I have often likened a perfectionistic family system to a steam-heating system which has a boiler but no pressure-relief valve to handle errors in the system. Without the pressure-relief valve these errors accumulate in the system until one day the boiler explodes and kills everyone within a ten-foot radius. Perfectionistic family systems are just like that.

If Dad and Mom are perfectionists, children learn they never do anything quite right. I had a client once who was a heart surgeon. He felt like a failure deep inside because he wasn't quite famous enough. He had graduated from medical school in the top ten percent of his class rather than the top five percent. His Vow, which was related to his having constantly "disappointed" his parents by not being perfect, was to become as perfect a doctor as he could possibly become. Sadly, there is no such thing as a perfect doctor. The result is that this man became perfectly miserable, as did all of those around him, including his friends and family. He had become so verbally critical and abusive that he was on the verge of losing his job and his family when he first came to see me.

As we worked through his painful, destructive perfectionism, it became clear that he was all bound up in distorted Christianity as well. He said, "My parents didn't abuse me. They were only doing what Christ commanded us to do — to become perfect like Him." What a trap this had become for him.

As I began to work with this surgeon, to delve into the childhood beliefs that were driving his abusive, imperfect, un-Christ-like behavior, he asked me if I could describe a perfect family system. He had read one of our books on dysfunctional families. I think he was hoping to catch me in some kind of mistake, which would be very possible since I'm not perfect. I thought for a long time, letting an uncomfortable silence hang in the air. Then I stared straight into his eyes and said, "A perfect family system has room for mistakes."

There was another long silence as he let my words settle inside of him and then he burst into tears. That was a critical moment in this surgeon's healing process. From there he was able to express years of outrage at the "hypocrisy of Christianity" as it had been practiced in his childhood home.

Months later he entered my office, sat down, smiled warmly and said, "I went to church last Sunday."

"The same church in which you were raised?" I asked.

"Yes," he answered. "It wasn't the church that was the problem."

SOME CHRISTIAN "BELIEF STRUGGLES"

All of us get caught up in our own belief distortions as we go through life. Each of us has our childhood vows that we are asked to uncover painfully and put to rest so we can become more holy. Each of us has moments of strength and moments of vulnerability. As we mature personally and spiritually, we flip-flop between extreme interpretations of our beliefs. The dynamic tension between extremes is what makes life painful, but also meaningful. If we were perfect, we wouldn't have to struggle, but none of us is perfect. We are all trying to improve our lives.

Love Your Neighbor As Yourself

Sometimes I think I'm doing this one well and sometimes not. Sometimes I give too much of myself and end up tired and resentful. When I stop and catch myself saying, "I don't want to care about anybody anymore," I know that it's time to back off and get some rest. But I don't always catch this right away. That's when I get into trouble and begin to feel used, tired, angry and scared.

At other times I don't give enough of myself and I start to feel guilty and ashamed. My guilt and shame tell me I'm out of balance and I need to care more for those around me. When I listen to that dynamic tension inside of me, I can get back on track pretty easily. When I don't, it's time to talk to another human being and get some perspective on myself. Sometimes looking in the mirror isn't enough. Sometimes the face of another person is the only reflection that will help.

At times I also get confused because I'm not so sure that I want to be around my "neighbor." Some people are obnoxious or intrusive. Some are abusive. Some are scary and some are boring. Does this mean that I must sit and listen endlessly to someone who is assaulting me, my sensibilities and my values? Or can I set appropriate limits with others and remove annoyance from my life.

At times like those I think back to how Christ handled those situations, and I rediscover that He was very firm and clear. Like the self-actualizing people described by Abraham Maslow, at times He challenged people and made them angry. He refused to compromise His values, yet He always respected the people to whom He related. When I think about the awesome combination of humility, power and respect for others that He consistently demonstrated, I know I have found someone who can teach me something I need to know without making me feel worthless because I don't know it. It feels good to have that kind of person in my life. Jesus was an incredible model for how to care for others without getting caught in their confusion and losing oneself in the process.

Suffer

I believe that Christ's suffering gave great dignity and meaning to our suffering. Not all Christians agree on the role of suffering in their theology. I grew up in a family where there was a lot of suffering and where religion was often used to justify that suffering. "We'll get our reward in heaven," someone would say. This line of thought was actually being used to avoid growing up. My parents used their religion, in part, to hide their shame and therefore to continue to emotionally abuse us.

I just don't believe that Jesus Christ meant us to use Him to hide behind so we could continue to be immature, frightened, ashamed and abusive. It simply doesn't make sense to me that He would condone abuse. Whenever I find myself suffering, I must be very careful in my examination of that suffering. Is it something over which I have some say? If it's physical pain, should I see a doctor or just ride it out? If it's emotional pain, should I try to improve the situation or endure it until it improves on its own?

I do not believe we should choose or create suffering for ourselves or others — there is enough on earth as it is. I do believe that our suffering has value but that to remain a victim of abuse in the name of suffering is not what being holy is about.

Honor Thy Father And Thy Mother

Some parents actually interpret this to mean that their children are meant to be tortured slaves. They think the Ten Commandments and Jesus Christ have given parents the right to do whatever they want to their children; their children must simply put up with it. Well, I don't believe Jesus meant this. If a parent is abusive to a child, then the child *honors* the parent by reporting the abuse so that both the parent and the child can get some help. To allow a person to abuse you is degrading both to you and to the person doing the abusing. The problem with young children is that they don't normally have the power or know how to deal with abusive parents. After all, without the parent the child would die, as Alice Miller so wisely pointed out.

What happens is that children fear abusive parents. They hope the parents will get better. They try to heal their parents so the parents can take care of them again. It is impossible to truly honor someone who is not honorable. Children can go through the motions, as the captives in the Nazi death camps must have done, but that isn't true honoring. True honoring is something else entirely.

The commandment "Honor thy father and thy mother" is one of the most widely quoted statements from the Bible in physically and sexually abusive homes. Research into the belief systems of child abusers is quite clear on this matter. Abusers *believe* that children have no human rights, that children can be treated like nonhumans, that children are to be feared and therefore severely controlled and punished, that children are evil and so on. There couldn't be a better quote from the Bible to be distorted in the mind of an abuser.

I believe we should honor our fathers and mothers, as long as we know what "honoring" means and what it does not mean. It does not mean disowning them because they were not perfect parents because no parents are perfect. It also does not mean that we must put up with ongoing abuse. It is illegal, immoral and un-Christian to abuse children.

Spare The Rod And Spoil The Child

Here again, it proves very enlightening to look at the extremes in trying to define the dysfunction. Children do need discipline, limits and boundaries. Spoiled children are no better off than physically abused children. One problem is that just about every form of physical discipline is actually physical abuse. It is unfortunate that we still don't do enough to teach young parents how to raise their children. There are so many humane methods of discipline that we know of today.

Another problem is that many parents view their children as "toys" or objects of entertainment. We set a bedtime for our kids, but then we let them stay up late to entertain us or to distract us from each other so that we don't have to face our own problems. We get them all riled up until they get out of control, then we lose control when we've had enough and rage and abuse these same kids. As they cry themselves to sleep, we can be heard muttering, "Those kids need to be disciplined more."

Well, I'll tell you what I believe: *Those* parents need to be disciplined more. They need more *internal* discipline so they can be consistent with their kids and take ownership of the way their kids have turned out.

There are all kinds of tortures that we once inflicted on infants and children in the name of good parenting, but, as Lloyd deMause noted, just because infants used to be salted and dunked in icewater to "harden" them centuries ago doesn't mean that it's okay by today's standards.

Surrender

In their moving documentary on Mother Teresa, Ann and Jeanette Petrie captured some remarkably simple and powerful statements from her. In explaining surrender, Mother Teresa said:

> To be where He wants you to be. If He puts you in the street, if everything is taken from you and suddenly you find yourself in the street, to accept to be in the street at that moment. Not for you to put yourself in the street. But to accept to be put there. This is quite different. To accept if God wants you to be in a palace, then to accept to be in the palace as long as you are not choosing to be in the palace. This is the difference . . . To accept all the people that come, the work that you happen to do. Today maybe you have a good meal, and tomorrow maybe you have nothing. There is no water in the pump. To accept.

> And to give whatever it takes. It takes your good name, it takes your health, it takes . . . yes, that's the surrender. *You are free then.* (Italics added.)

I try to live that way as much as I can, but it is very difficult. Like all human beings I don't like to admit that I have limits. To watch Mother Teresa working in the streets every day without burning herself out, and to sense the deep peace and happiness that she exudes as she lives out each day, is a spiritual experience in itself.

The idea of surrender is a controversial one these days. It is a key component of religion and spirituality, as well as of many systems of recovery from addictions. Many people feel it is also a big problem for those who are victimized repeatedly, such as women in abusive relationships. They argue that rather than learning to surrender these women need to become empowered so that they do not get hurt any longer. I couldn't agree more. Victims of ongoing abuse must become empowered so they can stop the abuse or get away from the abuser.

At the same time, anyone in an abusive relationship must first surrender to the fact that they are being abused and that up to now they have been unable to do anything about it. If we can't admit that there's a problem and that our previous efforts to solve it have failed, how will we ever change? If I don't know my fuel injector is broken, and if I'm not willing to admit that I can't fix it because I am mechanically illiterate, then my car simply won't run anymore. I'll be running everywhere but my car won't.

Each of us must surrender to something in the universe lest we risk believing that we are God. So even if you just admit that earthquakes or tornadoes are more powerful than you or that you can't control the weather, then at least there's some surrender there. The essence of addictiveness and nonspirituality would be to stand in your doorway as a tornado comes barreling toward your house, shaking your fist at it as you yell at it to go away — and actually believing that this approach will save you. I have seen tornadoes up close. It doesn't work.

The essence of spirituality and surrender is to know when to fight and when not to fight, as stated so elegantly in Reinhold Niebuhr's Prayer For Serenity: "To accept the things I cannot change, the courage to change the things I can, and the wisdom to know the difference." I don't believe that men or women who let themselves be victimized "in the name of surrender" are being healthy, but I do not believe that it is healthy to fight everybody on everything either. This is actually the reverse side of the same victim role and is no healthier. Powerful people pick their battles carefully; they know that some aren't worth fighting even though they may be "right." Jesus picked His battles very carefully. He said that we must give to Caesar what is Caesar's. His focus was on a much more important goal.

There are many more beliefs that can get painfully bound up in our Christianity. I encourage you to struggle with those beliefs that are getting you into trouble. Let yourself be challenged so you can continue to mature as adults and as Christians.

CHAPTER 8

Are Our Bodies Evil?

And the Word became flesh and dwelt among us, and we beheld His glory, the glory as of the only begotten of the Father, full of grace and truth.
John 1:14

Where We Got Off Track

I do not believe that our bodies are evil. I do believe it is a dangerous error to teach a person that her or his body is evil.

To understand why we believe what we believe about our bodies, I find it helpful to take a historical look at the issues. In his thoughtful book, *The History Of Childhood,* psychohistorian Lloyd deMause traced the evolution of child-rearing beliefs and practices from ancient times up to the present. In doing so, he noted that our own fears and lack of knowledge permitted horrific abuses of children that were culturally supported for centuries. These included the routine killing of both illegitimate children, which was done without regard for the infant's sex, and legitimate infants, which usually included most females and any infant who had any undesirable features or traits. He noted that in ancient Greece Polybius blamed the depopulation of the nation on the killing of legitimate children. The early Christians, noted deMause, were opposed to infanticide, but only marginally so. Other concerns took precedence over a practice so widely accepted that few people gave it a second thought.

The tales of horror from our historical past also include routine whippings, beatings, maiming, torturing, sexual abusing, emotional abusing, castrating and disfiguring of children. All of these at one time or another were culturally accepted by us, noted deMause, because of our own inner terror and lack of understanding of ourselves. In essence, parents of centuries ago projected their own unconscious fears, anxieties and shame onto children, whom they did not understand. Many of these overwhelming feelings had a sexual component to them, too.

Think about it. How many of us who become parents for the first time are free from this kind of projection? Very few, I should think. Imagine yourself as a young parent with a baby boy in your arms. He gets an erection, which is quite normal for baby boys. What are you to think? If you have even the slightest discomfort or shame about your own sexuality, it will be hard for you not to react to your own shame and project it onto your baby boy. At some deep, unconscious level you might think, "There is something wrong with my baby. He is somehow bad." You will try to put these thoughts out of your head, but if you are too afraid and ashamed to deal with your own sexual shame and discomfort, the thoughts will keep returning.

If there are other normal human things your baby does which make you feel inadequate as a new parent, like crying for no apparent reason, you will begin to build up an unconscious reservoir of projections toward your baby. Soon you will be abusing your baby boy "for his own good, to get the evil out of him," or some other such nonsense.

This is how it must have been historically, too. These confusing, nonadult little creatures who appeared to be irrational, unpredictable, frightening and even "filled with the devil" came into our lives. We were ill prepared to understand or raise them. So we did things to them that are now considered to be abuse.

Do you think parents today batter their infants because the parents are evil? I don't. I work with parents who batter and with adults who were battered. It is clear to me that parents batter because they get in over their heads and are too ashamed to ask for help. They don't know enough about infants and parenting to do otherwise. They batter because of their own shame and their own abusive histories. They batter because of ignorance and fear. They batter because of extreme stress. Many people batter because of their own misinterpretations of religious beliefs. None of them batter because they are evil as far as I know.

Our feelings about our bodies come from our culture, and our culture is passed down from one generation to the next in the blink of an eye. If cultures 2,000 years ago believed that infants and children were not human, and at the same time these cultures hurt children and used them sexually, then what was passed down were some disturbing notions about our bodies and our right to our own physical integrity. If we have been confused and even terrified by our sexual and emotional impulses for centuries, we will be projecting some odd notions onto our children as they grow up. This can be seen clearly when we look at Western religious notions about the body, the senses and sexuality since the early Christian era.

Body Alienation

As Christian theologian James Nelson pointed out in his groundbreaking book *Embodiment,* much of our confusion about sexuality and our bodies comes from the many "dualisms" of thought that have plagued humans for centuries. The most notorious of these is, of course, the mind-body dualism in which our cognitive, mental side is seen as separate from our physical, emotional side. For many great thinkers our cognitive side became synonymous with our spirituality, while our physical, emotional side was relegated to second-class citizenship. This interpretation leads us to the core belief or value judgment that the cognitive side is "better" or "holier" than the physical, emotional side. Our bodies and our emotions are seen as bothersome, cumbersome, troublesome and annoying at the very least. At the worst, this interpretation lets us feel that our bodies and emotions are actually evil.

Nelson noted a number of other painful, simplistic dichotomies that keep us stuck in childhood thinking, such as black/white, smart/stupid and good/bad. He then made an essential point that psychologists have known for some time: Whatever we do to dissociate ourselves from our feelings, our senses and thus our bodies will also cause us to dissociate from ourselves and others. Dissociation is just another way to say "alienated from." For what appears to me to be a majority of theologians and philosophers, alienation is another way to say "sin." Isn't that interesting? The real sin isn't to have a body and enjoy it respectfully and appropriately. The sin is when we deny that we have a body and become alienated from ourselves, others and, therefore, God.

In *The Divine Milieu,* Teilhard de Chardin wrote:

> In their struggle towards the mystical life, men have often succumbed to the illusion of crudely contrasting soul and body, spirit and flesh, as good and evil. But despite

> certain current expressions, this Manichean tendency has never had the Church's approval.

Rather than seeing the material world as an evil obstacle to our heightened spirituality, Teilhard saw created things as "footholds, intermediaries to be made use of, nourishment to be taken, sap to be purified and elements to be associated with us and borne along with us" as we make our spiritual journey. He then added: "In other words, the soul can only rejoin God after having traversed a specific path through matter — which path can be seen as the distance which separates, but it can also be seen as the road which links." And lastly, he said, "Thus it is not our business to withdraw from the world before our time; rather let us learn to orient our being in the flux of things."

What Does Mind-Body Separation Do To Us?

For centuries, theologians and the church tried to separate our bodies and our emotions from the rest of us. This has been perhaps one of the most damaging things that could have been done to us from a spiritual perspective. It also accounts for the inordinate amount of sexual addiction and sexual abuse that is acted out by lay people and the clergy alike. When we become alienated from our bodies, we become alienated from ourselves. When we become alienated from ourselves, we are no longer capable of relationship. We are alone, isolated, even schizoid. And when this happens, we become sexual and relationship offenders, hermits, or both.

It isn't a coincidence or a joke that every time a mass murderer is arrested, he is described as "a quiet man who kept to himself, kind of a loner." In my opinion, mass murderers are suffering from either a severe imbalance of brain chemicals, severe physical or emotional abuse in childhood, or both. The imbalance of brain chemicals interferes with their ability to perceive the world normally and therefore be in relationship with others. Certainly the severe abuse makes it difficult for them to be in relationship with others. So they grow up to engage in behaviors which are perverted, terrifying and disgusting.

Who can relate personally to the mind of a mass murderer? Probably another mass murderer, though we can get a sense of what that is like by simply getting in touch with our own alienation. When you are very worried about something, you may find it difficult to concentrate or to notice how you are feeling. You may be more accident-prone because you are so distracted. Your loved ones may comment that you "aren't yourself" and that it's hard to get close to you. You may snap at your children, grumble at your partner, lose sleep at night and make near-fatal errors at work — all because you're very worried about something.

If you learned as a child that expressing feelings was a sign of weakness or an occasion to be shamed by someone you love, then you will have a hard time expressing your feelings as an adult.

Psychologists have known for over 40 years that 80% of the emotional message conveyed to another person is done by our nonverbal language — our posture, tone of voice, facial expressions and so forth. Many people say they are expressing feelings because they talk about feelings, but this doesn't really work. To get a true emotional message across we have to *feel* the feelings. If you're sad, you need to let tears flow. If you're angry, you need to at least frown and raise your voice a little. Otherwise people won't know what you're trying to communicate, and you will become alienated from them.

Alienation also comes when we are so out of touch with our bodies that we don't know what we need or want. This can happen when we become so driven that we drive ourselves right into the ground. In modern terms, it's called "burnout," and it can literally kill us. We see a lot of helpers such as psychologists, ministers, doctors, counselors and teachers who get into burnout. Then we see them become so alienated from themselves that they don't even know they are physically and emotionally ill until the illness has become serious. After all, what's a little ulcer, a five-day headache or a "harmless" affair going to hurt?

With burnout also comes the inability to experience many feelings, including joy. Tired, aching, sick and joyless, we try to connect with our loved ones but find it nearly impossible. As we spiral downward into this bottomless pit of separation, our loved ones begin desperate attempts to help us while feeling lonely, isolated and angry themselves, but all we can do is lash out. Our behavior becomes in small but powerful ways perverted, terrifying and disgusting.

Alienation happens when we deny another person his or her identity, too. When we become separated from our emotions and our senses, we no longer have the full range of our humanity or our spirituality. This is how a sexual addict can justify seducing someone, having sex with them, telling them he or she loves them, then a few days later dumping them. The "object" of the addict's focus becomes a nonhuman, a set of walking genitals.

In war, commanders have known for centuries that the only way to get human beings to kill other human beings regularly is to somehow dehumanize the other human beings. That's why during World War II it was so necessary for us to speak of the Japanese as "Japs," the Germans as "Krauts" and the Italians as "Wops." That's why we spoke of African-Americans as "Niggers," because, if we afforded them the respect that is due all human beings, we wouldn't be able to live with ourselves for the way we were treating them.

Whenever a person says he hates a particular group of human beings and uses dehumanizing terms like "Micks," "fish-eaters," "Kikes," "poor white trash," "rich bastards," "scum," or "fags," then he has become alienated from himself, from his body, from his feelings, from other human beings, from his Christianity and from God. Adolf Hitler was a master at dehumanization of human beings. He even appealed to people's four-year-old comprehension of Christianity to justify the murder of millions of Jewish people. What I find personally terrifying is that this mindset is on its way back in many Western societies, including the United States and Germany. As much as some of us will probably hate to hear this, every time we condemn someone because they believe in Islam, Buddhism, Judaism, Catholicism, Episcopalianism, Presbyterianism or the Big Bang theory of the universe, we are joining the forces of intolerance, fear, superstition, hatred and evil in the world. Nobody said you had to believe these other beliefs, but to condemn others for using their God-given brains to think and wonder does not feel like something that Jesus Christ would do.

WHAT DID CHRIST TEACH US ABOUT OUR BODIES?

Christ Taught Us That Our Bodies Are Holy And Have Dignity

He did this simply by being a human being. If He had come to us in the form of a ghost or a spirit only, the message would have been very different, wouldn't it? By having a human body, He gave dignity to the human body. By displaying human emotions, He gave dignity to human emotions. By being subjected to temptation, He let us know that being subjected to temptation is part of being human. By associating with what society defines as many of its more flawed members, He let us know in no uncertain terms that every human being is equal in the eyes of God. We in all our flawed humanity are capable of having worth, dignity, value and holiness.

Think about bodies. Different cultures have different reactions to the human body. A large portion of white middle-class American culture is absolutely nuts when it comes to the body. We are ashamed, disgusted, afraid, obsessed and distorted when it comes to bodies. It's all that many of us think about. We focus on bodies. We glorify bodies. We hate bodies — our own in particular. It's sad that we do that. It doesn't have to be this way. We can change our culture.

Christ Taught Us That It Is Okay To Have All Of Our Feelings

In our distorted, four-year-old thinking, many of us have seen Jesus Christ in a very childish way. We have tried to rob Him of His dignity and worth by assuming He did not have all of the feelings that we mere humans have. If He was just a "pretend human" who wasn't subject to the same joy, pain, loneliness, fear, despair and anger that we are, it would have meant that His time on earth was a hoax. I don't believe He represented a hoax or a trick. I believe that He really got angry, felt hurt, felt betrayed, despaired, felt alone, felt sad and enjoyed Himself and his friends.

That's why the frightened reaction to Martin Scorsese's film, *The Last Temptation Of Christ*, was so sad. Many people I know who saw the film came out of it with a much-deepened commitment to their Christian faith and with a renewed sense of appreciation for what Christ endured while on earth. If Jesus hadn't actually been tempted to give up his suffering and simply lead a normal life like those around Him, what would have been the point? Jesus had to be human, and He had to have a full range of human feelings for it to all work out the way it was meant to.

Because of His humanity I don't have to apologize in that I feel shame or hurt or anger or loneliness. I know that I must try to act with respect for myself and others, but I also know that I don't have to feel bad just because I feel something.

Jesus Taught Us To Care For Our Bodies

Your body is an important part of your identity while you are here on earth. Who we are and how we behave is very much affected by the condition of our bodies. For example, if you do things to hurt your brain, like ingesting dangerous chemicals or tainted food or water, your brain can begin to act up and cause you to act up. People often abuse others terribly while under the influence of chemicals but return to normal, loving behavior when they stop using chemicals. Don't think for a minute that your spirituality and your capacity to love are not affected by your body. It makes no sense at all to separate them.

St. Thomas Aquinas, who made enormous contributions to Catholic theology, was known as a highly logical, intellectual man. His contributions were logical and intellectual. Aquinas was also obese, allegedly weighing over 400 pounds. He had to have a special desk built so he could stand up while he worked, since he was unable to sit down for long periods of time. I realize that his addiction to food was one of his human flaws and I do not mean to diminish the importance of his intellectual contributions because of it. I do wonder whether his theology might have been different had he taken better care of himself and had he been more aware of his body and his feelings rather than just his mind.

The Temple Of The Spirit

My colleagues who are neuropsychologists or physiological psychologists tell me that our understanding of the brain and its interaction with the rest of the body is advancing so fast that the textbooks must be rewritten every few years. With every bit of new knowledge that we acquire, it becomes clearer that our bodies are important determiners of how we think, feel and act. We can choose to be ashamed of our bodies or we can choose to be in awe of what a marvelous creation the body is. Science and theology complement each other well in this way.

Each of us is born with a certain kind of body. Some of us are tall, some short, some prone to put on weight, others prone to be thin. Some have energetic bodies and some have bodies that are subject to depression. Most characteristics in nature are normally distributed, which means there is a whole range of physical features, shapes and sizes that make up the human race. You didn't choose the body that your parents' genes constructed for you so you shouldn't have to apologize — have shame — about your body. Healthy, spiritual parents can and do love each of their children for their uniqueness as much as for their family similarities. Healthy parents who have dealt with their own "body embarrassment" will not need to shame you about your body. Healthy parents who have come to accept and like their bodies will automatically be teaching you to accept and like your body, too.

If you feel the need to challenge what is evil in our society when it comes to bodies, challenge the role that advertising plays in your family's life. Watch less television. Discuss with your family the powerful, unconscious messages that bombard us every day until we can't think straight. Discuss the messages that say we are less than everyone else if we aren't at least a "seven" on a ten-point scale of beauty. Talk about how shaming and alienating these messages are — how they keep us from getting close to certain people either because of how they look or because of how we look.

I don't recall anywhere in the New Testament where Christ said only the beautiful people will enter the kingdom of heaven. Families that have a lot of body shame are in pain and need to heal. The mistake, the error, the "sin" in these families is that of the alienation, self-disgust and shame that are passed on to the children. We need to let our kids know that they are loved no matter what, as Christ loved us. We need to help our children care for their bodies by caring for our own. We need to teach them social skills, including appropriate grooming, because these are part of belonging to a community. We also need to let them know by our behavior that every single human being's body is truly the temple of her or his spirit.

CHAPTER 9

Sex, Sexual Abuse And Christianity

For this reason a man shall leave his father and mother and be joined to his wife, and the two shall become one flesh, so then they are no longer two, but one flesh.

Mark 10:7-8

People used to be horrified when the rare news story broke about the good dad who was caught sexually molesting his daughter. Some people even wanted to believe him when he said the little girl seduced him because it was too scary to admit that what we believe we're seeing in another person is sometimes not the truth at all.

Those rare news stories aren't that rare anymore because we are at last awakening to the true extent of sexual abuse in America. We now know that roughly 28% of all women in America will be physically sexually abused by the time they reach age 21; and that about 16% of men will be, too. We know that a large percentage of that abuse will happen in the child's home. Much of it will be perpetrated by someone who knows the child — Dad, Stepdad, Mom, Stepmom, babysitter, Grandpa, Grandma, Uncle, Aunt, friend of the family or other relative. According to the American Humane Association there were 391,200 reported cases of child sexual abuse in 1989. Of those, 74% of the victims were girls and 26% were boys. The perpetrator was the father in 30% of the cases and the mother in 10% of the cases. In 75% of the cases, the abused child knew the offender — often a relative or friend of the family.

We know that nonphysical forms of sexual abuse are even more common. These include leering or staring at the child, visually undressing the child, inappropriate nudity, lack of sexual boundaries, being overly modest and ashamed of one's body so children also learn that shame, objectifying a person's sexuality, not accepting the child because he is a boy or because she is a girl. We know that 80% of women who go to inpatient treatment for alcoholism or other chemical dependency are survivors of physical sexual abuse. We know that 90% of female prostitutes were physically sexually abused as little girls.

What's even scarier is a discovery many clinicians have made since the early 1980s. The likelihood of incest happening in a family is greater in certain types of religious families than in the population at large. The Jimmy Swaggerts and the Jim and Tammy Bakkers of the world — people who put themselves in positions of moral leadership or who claim to have a special religious calling but who are actually very addictive and even sociopathic — are just the tip of the sexually dysfunctional iceberg. The Catholic priest who abuses altar boys is just the tip of the iceberg. The Baptist minister who has numerous sexual affairs with members of his flock is just the tip of the iceberg.

The Religion/Sexual Shame Connection

This is nothing new. Literature is filled with the Elmer Gantrys who act out compulsive sexuality in the context of religion. What is new is our discovery of the extent of sexual abuse and acting out in this country and of the way it can be so closely tied in with religion. For those of you who are already getting defensive and angry because I am tying together religion and sexual abuse, please remember that I said it "can be" tied in with religion. Certainly, sexual abuse happens in families from every income level, from various religions, in nonreligious families and many other types of families. Incest and sexual abuse know no socioeconomic or religious boundaries.

Yet there is a religion/sexual abuse connection. How could there not be? Think about it. We have some very sick notions about sex in America, some of which go back even before our Puritan roots in early New England and some of which we have conjured up all by ourselves in the late 20th century. From our ancestors we have picked up and incorporated the core belief that sex is dirty, evil, bad, wrong and just plain nasty. We can tolerate it for purposes of procreation, but let's not enjoy it. A 1991 cover story in *U.S. News & World Report* was entitled "Sex And Religion: Churches, The Bible And Furor Over Modern Sexuality." We are obviously still confused and upset by sex.

In *Embodiment*, theologian James Nelson noted that "To the Hebrews sexuality was a good gift from God." Later denial of the goodness of the body came in part from "Persian beliefs which correlated salvation with sexual restriction." I strongly encourage you to read his book, which gives an elegant history of the development of our religious beliefs about the body and sexuality from antiquity to the present. What is clear to me as I ponder all of this is that if sex is bad, then of course our bodies must also be bad. It's just a hop, a skip and a jump until we believe that it's bad to be male or female. From there it's inevitable to say, "I am bad."

There's something else in our culture that gets us all messed up about sexuality. First we have our sexual shame, which is fostered by many American religious leaders who have yet to grow up and face their own sexual issues. On top of that is the way our American advertising firms use sex to sell everything from cigarettes and beer to water pumps and trips to the Caribbean. This produces a terrible sexual double bind or double message: Sex is shameful, but it's also titillating and exciting and devoid of any human emotion or relationship. In fact, if many of our beer commercials on television are correct, all we have to do is get a bunch of women in bikinis, a bunch of beer, a bunch of loud obnoxious guys, some sand and a ball of some kind, and we can cure for all eternity the misery, pain, sadness, injustice, poverty, famine, disease and immorality in the world, and we can do it all in 15 seconds. If only it were that easy.

Popular talk-show host Geraldo Rivera wrote a book with a sexually suggestive title, *Exposing Myself,* in which he outlined his sexual exploits in a sensational way without discretion. Colleagues of mine who specialize in working with survivors of sexual abuse and with sexual addiction note that the way Geraldo conducts himself on his programs are exploitive. "He feels scary," one recovering client of ours noted. Under the guise of exposing abuses in society, Geraldo appears to me to be exploiting the victims of sexual abuse by the way he conducts himself during his show. On one segment, for example, he knelt dramatically at the feet of an abuse survivor and wiped her tears with his handkerchief in a way that sent chills down the spines of the recovering sex addicts and sex abuse survivors in my therapy groups.

As Wendy Kaminer begrudgingly admitted in *I'm Dysfunctional, You're Dysfunctional,* her critique of the recovery movement, talk shows can be "instructive in ways they intend" on occasion. I believe they may have their place in society if conducted with boundaries and respect, but many of us are so damaged already that we don't get what's happening when we're being "slimed." We are drawn to this kind of offensive performance rather than repulsed by it, so the show continues successfully. A show like this also exploits the voyeuristic tendencies of so many of us repressed Americans who seem to "need to watch." The American public watches, day in and day out, which is why Geraldo does it. He is making a darned good living because we are disgusted with, intrigued by, addicted to, ashamed of and infinitely desirous of SEX. I would much rather have people look at tasteful, artistic photographs of nude people than watch a show like that where their baser emotions and minds are manipulated along with their genitals.

We have television evangelist Jimmy Swaggert crying shamelessly on national television after "getting caught with his pants down" with a prostitute for the first time. Millions of people forgave him instantly. Apparently they didn't know that sexual addiction is a serious disorder and a difficult and long-term problem to treat. Nor did they know that being able to turn tears on and off like a faucet is part of the disease. A few years later we found Jimmy Swaggert getting caught with his pants down a second time, but this time there were no crocodile tears. He wasn't about to try that old crying stunt again. This time he dealt with the problem head-on. He simply claimed that God told him to tell all of us to shut up. I don't know how religious comedian David Letterman is, but he or the writers for his talk show made a lot of sense to me on this one. He asked, "If God is really talking directly to Jimmy Swaggert, don't you think He's been telling Jimmy to lay off the prostitutes?"

It is we who support and allow this kind of religious mockery and ignorance. We are afraid to think, we are afraid to grow up and we are scared to death of our own sexuality. Getting titillated about sex by a television Elmer Gantry or talk-show host, getting titillated about sex by television and magazine ads, and then being disgusted and ashamed about pure, healthy human sexuality makes no sense at all. It is, to use a phrase coined by Virginia Satir, crazymaking. I don't trust people who rant and rave about the evils of sex. Too often they are also the sexual perpetrators who have hurt my clients. Or they are the sexual victims who hurt but who fear healing and therefore will pass their sexual dysfunction on to their children, who will pass it on to theirs, all "in the name of God or Jesus Christ."

A Religion/Incest Example

The way we practice our religion can also enter into the sexual abuse picture. Because incest is so difficult for people to comprehend, let's take a closer look at how religion and incest might be connected. Suppose that as a child you were given messages that you were very bad, that your normal sexual urges were bad, that you were not nearly as smart as your brother or sister, that you were not as special as they were, that you had somehow disappointed Dad or Mom, that you weren't interesting enough and so on.

Now let's say that as you reach adolescence, when you're supposed to start the scary process of dating, you don't feel good enough about yourself to date and you don't. You go into young adulthood without having had any emotional dating experiences so you don't know what you like, who you like or how you feel in these situations.

Then you fall in love and get married to the first person you meet as a young adult. The two of you are naive and inexperienced. Perhaps both of your families had a lot of sexual shame. Nobody ever talked about sex, what it's for, where it fits into the big picture. Because your parents were terrified and ashamed of their own sexuality, they taught you to feel the same way about yours. So those normal, healthy, holy and sacred feelings of sexuality that you began to have confused the heck out of you.

You and your new young spouse didn't know what sex was about, so the two of you were like little kids literally groping around in the dark. You didn't have the emotional tools to talk to each other. That sexual shame kept rearing its ugly head and neither of you knew what to do with it. So you did nothing. You "had sex" in the dark. You changed clothes in the dark because of your embarrassment. You were both frustrated, miserable and scared. Then you had a child.

Which of the following do you think would be less threatening to an adult who grew up in a sexually dysfunctional home?

1. Trying to work out your sexual relationship with another adult, such as your spouse?
2. Acting out your sexuality with a vulnerable child?

Right. It's less threatening for an emotionally immature adult to act out their sexuality with a child.

Next question: If I believe that sex is evil, dirty and awful, won't I just become totally asexual/nonsexual? Perhaps. But our sexuality is a part of us that is closely related to our identity and our spirituality. We can try to deny that we are sexual, just as we can try to deny that we have feelings or bodies, but it won't do any good. So what will happen instead is that our sexuality will "come out sideways." It will be expressed in an unhealthy way.

Your young spouse, who is extremely uncomfortable with sex, is just plain happy that your sex life involves a clumsy "quickie" in the dark once every couple of weeks. During this time neither of you speaks or makes eye contact which makes it even yuckier and more shameful for both of you.

Next question: Do many incest perpetrators actually believe that their sexual relationship with their child is "special" and that it can even have religious significance for them and the child? Yes. When we are emotionally immature, we can make all kinds of connections between things that are not connected at all. Piaget called this "syncretic thought." We can believe it is our child's job to take care of us emotionally, that he or she is supposed to be our buddy, pal or companion. Those are emotional boundaries that are being violated. The sexual ones are right behind them.

As your child grows older you find all of those sexual feelings that would normally be directed at your spouse being directed at your child. You try to push those thoughts and feelings away but they won't go away. You begin to fantasize about your child. Your child's innocence and vulnerability don't signal you the way they would signal a healthy parent. To a healthy parent, their child's innocence and vulnerability represent a "biological stop sign" that says "I'm a child. You can't have sex with me." Healthy parents heed the stop sign. Spiritually and sexually shamed parents see the stop sign but to them it says "Go." That's sort of how the disease of incest works.

In her thoroughly professional review of incest literature for *Lear's* magazine, Heidi Vanderbilt cites the work of Finkelhor and Williams of the University of New Hampshire. They identified several types of incest depending upon the motive. Some of the incestuous fathers they interviewed acted out because they were angry at their daughter or someone else. Others had regressed back to adolescence, while others were purely preoccupied with sex. Some fantasized having sex with someone else while they molested their daughters. Others were emotionally dependent men who were basically getting from their daughters what they should have been getting from other adults, particularly their spouse.

Sexuality And Spirituality

Our sexuality and our spirituality are so closely intertwined that it is at times difficult to separate them, yet we have tried to separate them for centuries. This separation of our sexuality from the rest of our "self" is a perversion that has resulted in centuries of other perversions. I am thus very relieved to see this attitude gradually changing in America. Even if we choose to be celibate for religious or other reasons, we are still sexual beings.

Our sexuality is not just our genital, reproductive urges, although it includes these. It is also an expression of our maleness or femaleness, of our level of comfort with our bodies, of our creative life force, of our energy and our spirit. It expresses love, communication and intimacy between two people. To imply that our sexuality is bad and should be suppressed is simply to say that we are bad and should be suppressed.

Some of you may be thinking, "He's saying that sex is everything and that everyone should engage in genital sex all of the time." Please reread the last two paragraphs if that's what you think. I didn't say that at all. I said that even if you choose to be celibate, you are still a sexual being. What you choose to do with your sexuality is just that — it is a choice.

For those of you who have not chosen to be celibate, I ask that you look at where sexual behavior fits into your life. Healthy, spiritual people who love each other find that their sexual life, rather than getting boring over the years, is an important part of their communication and the celebration of their relationship. Catherine Johnson pointed this out in her excellent research-based book on happy couples entitled *Lucky In Love.*

Sexual intercourse and orgasm are actually a beautiful physical metaphor for life and death itself, as Peter Koestenbaum pointed out in *Existential Sexuality*. We come together, join and almost fuse both physically and emotionally. We share a physical and emotional ecstasy unparalleled in our sensory experience. Then we must separate again. We don't want to separate but we must and so we do. During a healthy sexual experience, we become highly vulnerable and open to another human being, to ourselves and to the universe. People who have an open stance toward life in general and who can be vulnerable when it is safe, do not have sexual dysfunctions that I know of, except in the case of physical problems. Likewise, people who are open and vulnerable in their lives do not have a great fear of death.

People who are sexually repressed and blunted are terrified of their feelings in general, not just their sexual ones. They are afraid of the risks involved in nonsexual intimacy. Being unable to experience feelings clearly and being afraid to risk intimacy make the even more mature and abstract task of being spiritual difficult for many people.

Having a spiritual experience requires that we let go of our control, then surrender to what is more powerful than us. We open ourselves up to creation and become vulnerable and powerful all at the same time. We feel at one with creation. We have a tearful, joyous awe and wonder about the unknowable in the universe. We are afraid and unafraid in the same breath, and we are infinitely humbled by the experience. Do you see the connection between spirituality and sexuality? What I just wrote could be used to describe a spiritual experience that you had while in church, while looking up at the star-filled night sky, while in a caring conversation with a friend or while having sexual intercourse with your partner.

Watch a truly romantic love scene in a film that has no nudity but that is filled with understated passion and tasteful erotic energy, and you will see sexuality that is beautiful, powerful and spiritual. Notice what you feel as you watch. Notice what a risk it is for two adults of equal power to approach each other sexually. It's not at all like a sexual offender approaching a child or forcing himself or herself onto a less powerful adult. Healthy sexuality between two adults of equal power is a wonderful, holy celebration of life itself.

WHAT IS SEX?

There are actually two questions to be answered here. One is about sexual reproduction and the other is about sexual communication.

Sexual Reproduction

Sexual reproduction is one of the most ingenious mechanisms in creation. There are animals that reproduce asexually by simply dividing in two or by having both male and female genitals and simply fertilizing themselves, but our form of reproducing ourselves allows an infinite number of combinations and recombinations of genetic material. This ensures our genetic flexibility and therefore our survivability on the planet.

How did our form of sexual reproduction evolve? One biologist has conjectured that billions of years ago a one-celled animal was "eating" another one-celled animal and didn't quite "digest" its prey. The result was that part of its prey's genetic material became incorporated into its own genetic material. Perhaps this made the predator and its cell lines more resistant to extinction. Billions of years later, we have these little cells with little tails all swimming madly to try to fuse their genetic material with another cell. It is my own conjecture that our feelings of "sexual hunger" for each other may have evolved from this initial "dietary hunger" of one little animal for another.

So here we are in the 1990s. We reach puberty, our bodies start producing large amounts of reproductive hormones and we change shape. Then we start taking a great deal of interest in each other in ways we never did before. If you ever have any doubts about how amazing creation is, just take a course in biology. It's incredible to think about it. It's sad, too. It's sad to think that God designed this intricate, complicated process for our reproduction, made it evolve gradually over billions of years so we would have some fascinating things to study while in college, and He made it extremely pleasurable so we would be sure to do it a lot, and then we come along with our grandiose godlike notions and try to make the whole process evil. If someone you know really thinks that sex is evil, ask them to talk to God about it. Maybe God will change creation just for them.

Sexual reproduction is what we are supposed to be doing. There is nothing wrong with it in the context of a loving relationship. It's time for Christians to grow up and face the fact that it is *we* who have been "evil" with our sexual shame, sexual repression and sexual guilt. Sex isn't bad. Our fear of it, of ourselves and of being spiritual is what makes this normal human function seem bad to many of us.

Yes, people can do great harm to each other by acting out their pain sexually. Yes, sex is exploited in this country, but do we have to be slaves to our own fearful extremes?

Sexual Communication

When our clients are beginning to sort out the problems in their relationships, the issue of sex often comes up as a major one. In fact, we ask all of our clients about their sexuality early in therapy because sexuality is an extremely sensitive barometer for how the rest of us is functioning. In a relationship, this is especially true. I believe that sexuality is related to, or is a subset of, two parts of us:

1. Our Sensuality
2. Our Intimacy

Sensuality

In *Reason And Emotion,* British philosopher John MacMurray wrote that we have woefully neglected the education of our senses. He argued that this neglect of the sensory world in favor of the mental world of logical thought is dangerous:

> The senses are the gateways of our awareness. They are the avenues along which we move into contact with the world around us. Without this sensuous awareness of the world, no consciousness and no knowledge of any kind is possible, for human beings at least. Even our knowledge of God is only possible through the awareness of the world which our senses provide.

The most common and successful treatment for sexual dysfunctions of all kinds includes a core of exercises designed to get people to educate their senses. Each of the partners must learn to see, hear, smell, taste and touch, in nonsexual ways, long before they are allowed to be physically sexual with each other during the course of treatment. They must learn to notice what they find pleasurable and what they don't find pleasurable. They must learn to communicate with their partner about nonsexual sensuality before communicating their sexual likes and dislikes. This sensory-education-awareness process has a nice side benefit, too. It takes time and it therefore slows down the couple's sexual encounter, making it much more intimate, personal, caring and spiritual.

God gave us our senses not only so we could gather information about the world but also for pleasure. That's what "pleasing to the senses" means. It is not evil to enjoy the sight of fresh flowers in a vase on your kitchen table. It is not evil to enjoy the smell of freshly baked bread. It is not evil to enjoy the cozy patter of rain falling on your roof. Life is a combination of pleasure and discomfort. It should not be all discomfort, and it should not be all pleasure. There needs to be a balance. Enjoying our sensuality is part of what our Creator intended by allowing us to feel pleasure and joy. If He hadn't wanted us to feel pleasure, he wouldn't have wired it into our brains.

Body awareness and sensory awareness are very important for another reason. They are the cure for the dissociative problems that I discussed in the previous chapter. Learning to zero in on our own body states and then learning to communicate our needs to a trusted partner, are parts of the cure for alienation and dissociation.

Our genital sexuality is simply one part of our much broader sensuality. We certainly experience sex through our senses. But our sensuality is much more than just sexual. People get shut down to the point that they don't appreciate anything they take in through their senses. Then they wonder why their sexual organs don't work. Retrain your eyes, ears, tastebuds, nose and skin to take in the world around you. After that, see how your sex life has improved. But remember you may have to overcome some unhealthy guilt that tells you it is bad to be pleased. Just think of the flowers on the table or the freshly baked bread and that will help to melt away the guilt.

Intimacy

Even more confusing to many of us is the fact that our sexuality is part of a much larger world of intimacy. It is easy to get the relationship between the two confused. You find yourself attracted to each other and begin a relationship. Relationships go in stages.

In the first stage, you are both blinded to differences. Everything is rosy. You are on top of the world. There are no fights or disagreements. It feels as if your partner is fulfilling your lifelong dream — to have someone in whom you can become totally absorbed, who will always completely understand you and meet all of your needs without you ever having to ask. It feels as if your new love will be able to heal every last hurt and wound inside of you, but this is an illusion, as Teilhard de Chardin explained in *Human Energy.*

The next stage is one of dynamic tension which promises much deeper intimacy to the couple who face the challenge. You begin this stage with the unconscious realization that getting completely lost in another person is not only scary but unhealthy. Suddenly all sorts of conflicts bubble up to the surface. You flip to the other extreme and wonder why you ever got into the relationship in the first place. Your partner's little habits that were once so "charming" quickly lose their charm. You may fight about "trivial" things and secretly feel like you are childish and petty, but these "little" issues are the backdrop for much deeper ones. You may feel disappointed to find that your partner isn't perfect, and that your partner won't be able to meet all of your needs. You may feel secretly betrayed. Your partner isn't the perfect Dad or Mom that you needed.

Enter sex. As sex is a metaphor for life and death, it is also a reflection of the level of intimacy that we share. During this important "struggle phase" of our relationship, we may begin to do something different with our sexuality. We may use it to act out our anger and disappointment by withdrawing from our partner, or worse, by comparing our partner to someone from our past. We may use it as a distraction to avoid the conflicts all together. Some people say that their sex life is "fantastic" but that every other part of their relationship is in a shambles. This is a clear case in which sex has become a substitute for real intimacy.

What is loving, intimate communication? Part of intimacy is intellectual, in which we share our thoughts, beliefs and knowledge. Part of intimacy is behavioral, in which we share things like chores, hobbies and the like. Part of it is social, in which we share ourselves with friends. The part that confuses many people is that of emotional communication — sharing feelings. It is absolutely essential to a relationship that both people be able to share feelings, including the ones that aren't so easy to share.

It is a very intimate act to tell your partner that his breath is really bad and that you would appreciate it if he would brush his teeth. If this is a constant problem and you tell yourself that it isn't important enough to mention, someday you'll explode and tell him in a very hurtful way.

It is a very intimate act to tell your partner that you appreciate her and are deeply grateful to have her in your life. It is as big a risk to say that, as it is to tell her that it makes you angry when she takes your things and doesn't return them. When we share our true feelings with someone, it is an act of love.

Now think about this. If you don't share your day-to-day feelings with each other because it's too risky or difficult, how on earth will you be able to communicate with each other sexually? You won't. You will have a mediocre sex life at best. It is very possible that you will secretly resent your partner or feel deep shame about yourself, all because neither of you is willing to be vulnerable with each other as you tell each other what you need sexually.

Healthy couples eventually take the huge, intimate risk of becoming emotionally vulnerable to each other so their hurts and wounds from the past can be healed. This can only happen if each person maintains his or her separate identity in the process. It is as important to be separate in a relationship as it is to be together. As a couple takes these deeper emotional risks, their sexuality becomes firmly embedded in a much broader context of separateness, dignity, compassion and emotional closeness. Our sexuality needs to become a humble yet ecstatic part of something bigger — our love for each other.

Christian Sexuality

I believe that Christian sexuality is holy sexuality. Christ saw the dignity in every person He encountered. He respected their humanity without question. He valued honesty and integrity in relationships. He deplored fraud and hypocrisy. He wept for us. He showed us His vulnerability. He showed us His strength. He prayed for us. He enjoyed us. He celebrated with us. He nurtured us. He bonded with us. He loved us.

Holy sexuality is like that. It is honest. It is dignified. It is fun. It is passionate. It doesn't have to be a perfect "performance." It is caring and loving. It is not domineering. It is a celebration of life. It is nurturing. It is a risk. It is comfortable. It requires vulnerability and strength at the same time, and it is one very important part of human intimacy.

So please, if you catch yourself believing that your sexuality is evil or dirty, reconsider. Re-examine that belief. Because that belief in our culture is responsible for sexual abuse, sexual addiction, rape, incest and countless other forms of human pain that will all cease when we learn to accept our sexuality as a holy part of us. Whether you choose to be celibate or not, you are still a sexual being. It is part of your body. Hating a part of yourself that God gave you is just the opposite of Christ's teaching.

CHAPTER 10

The Pharisees And Hypocrites: Shame, Fear, Prejudice And Ignorance

Judge not, and you shall not be judged. Condemn not, and you shall not be condemned.

Luke 6:37

Sometimes I'll just scan through a book, looking at section headings and chapter titles so I can get a picture of the overall themes of a book. If you have one of those Bibles that has interpretive headings on every section, try it sometime. As I scan through the first four books of the New Testament, I am struck by a number of insights. For example, Jesus told a lot of parables. He did a lot of teaching. A lot of people were excited to follow Him. He hung around anybody and everybody.

Huston Smith wrote that Jesus ". . . liked people, and they liked him in return . . . He felt the appeal of people, whether they were rich or poor, young or old, saints or sinners." When I read those words, they sound nice, but when I actually visualize what this Man must have been like, I am awestruck. What an example He was!

Huston Smith also wrote that Jesus hated injustice because of what it did to children, and that most of all Jesus "hated hypocrisy because it hid a man even from himself and precluded that wealth of fellowship He sought to build among men." As I scan through the New Testament, I see numerous references by Jesus to the hypocrisy that He saw in the religious leaders of His time. In fact, it was their attempt to entrap Jesus that prompted Him to give us the Two Great Commandments:

> You shall love the Lord your God with your whole heart, with your whole soul, and with your whole mind.
>
> You shall love your neighbor as yourself.
>
> Mark 12:30-31

Without a doubt, these are profound and important words. The fascinating thing about them is that they were very controversial in Christ's time. They must have angered the religious experts who were trying to trap Him. The words were too simple, too direct — and much too difficult to carry out. It was much easier to pray publicly for all to see and admire than to care for a crippled beggar or prostitute or foreigner. The First Great Commandment might be okay. If I am a hypocrite, it would be easy to believe that I have a special relationship with God Almighty that "lesser men" don't have, simply to feed my own narcissism. But The Second? Love your neighbor as yourself? That was a bit much. I am better than my neighbor. See how I fast in public and how I broadcast all of my good works?

The other thing that interests me about these 27 words is to see what has happened to them over the 2,000 years we have had to think about them. On the positive side, we have become more humane in many ways, despite what seem like hopeless social problems in our nation today. I believe that as a culture we do treat each other better than people were treated 2,000 years ago. On the down side, many of us verbally agree that these 27 words are how we should live but then we don't live that way.

I know we are human and we aren't perfect, but it scares me to see all of us professing to be Christians or Jews or Muslims or whatever, then not living at all according to those professed beliefs. It saddens me to see a frightened, confused mother and father drive their gay teenage son to suicide because they don't understand homosexuality and because our churches have forgotten what Christ's love was really like. It saddens me to see us fear and hate people who don't look like us or who don't believe what we believe. Yes, we need law and order in our societies, but we also need compassion and understanding. Law and order are agentic. Compassion and understanding are communal. That was Jesus' primary message. That's what He said with those 27 words.

We Need Our Shame

Americans have been struggling with the concept of shame for the past several years, largely due to Gershen Kaufman's work. The consensus seems to be that we have all been shamed far too much by our parents and that we need to break free of that shame once and for all. If you have read ours or anyone else's books on painful families, you already know that we agree there is too much *abusive shame* in American families.

Abusive shame passes freely and effortlessly from one generation to the next, resulting directly or indirectly in alcoholism, incest, physical and emotional violence, poverty and excruciating pain for everyone in its path. Linda and I try to help people deal with this abusive shame every working day.

While recovery from child abuse requires rejecting unhealthy shame, it doesn't mean that we get to stop being *accountable.* Shame, or embarrassment, is a feeling. All human feelings have a purpose, a value and an importance. The healthy shame that we feel lets us know we are not God. It lets us know we have limitations. It lets us know there is still room for improvement. It lets us know we are alienated. The only being who doesn't need to improve is a perfect being — God.

So here we are in 1993. We have survived the Industrial Revolution partially, although our planet is gasping for air. We have survived centuries of regional wars which culminated in two world wars, shameful holocausts, a cold war and hundreds of recent and current regional wars. Thus far we have avoided a worldwide nuclear holocaust.

In Western industrialized nations we have irradicated most of the biological plagues and diseases that haunted us for centuries. Some of these, of course, will return if we aren't careful about how we care for each other, and new ones, such as AIDS, will no doubt continue to emerge. We can transplant organs with fair ease and we are on the brink of being able to change a person's genetic destiny.

We can land on the moon and return safely. We can fly by jet anywhere in the world or call just about anyone on the planet by telephone. We have the capacity to produce vast amounts of food with a minimum of labor; we can build automobiles with robots instead of people; we have computers that can perform calculations, that might have taken centuries just a few short years ago, in minutes. With our telescopes and microwave detection devices we have witnessed the beginning of creation known as the Big Bang. Through archaeological exploration we have been able to peek back into our own human beginnings thousands of years ago, which lets us feel more at one with our primitive ancestors and therefore with ourselves as a race.

Over the centuries, and in every culture on earth, we have produced works of music, art and literature that are so exquisite they are described as heavenly. Through the arts, we have chronicled and immortalized the hopes, dreams, fantasies, tragedies, successes, failures, drives, motives and experiences of our peoples around the planet in ways that are mysterious, inspiring and powerful. We have even built machines that can create works of art by themselves, mimicking our creative brain pathways with silicon chip pathways of their own.

We are an incredible, marvelous, wonderful, inventive, clever, poetic, compassionate, creative, spiritual species. Because of that, and because we are fallible human beings, we sometimes get so taken with ourselves that we begin to believe we are God. That's when we become an ugly, deceitful, arrogant, nasty, abusive, terrifying and evil species. Believing that we are gods alienates us from the very God in whom we profess to believe. At that point we become like little children who are left too long without supervision by healthy adults. We become frightened, domineering, jealous, intolerant and cruel with each other. We act as if we don't have thousands of years of religion, culture, science, technology and knowledge under our belts. We become like our early ancestors — barbarians.

I get scared about American society sometimes. Sometimes I am ashamed of us. For example, although this attitude is gradually changing, many of us still like to think of ourselves as the moral leaders of the world. We have this notion that we Americans are 260 million generous, loving, practical, caring, democratic, Christian folks who have all the right answers for the rest of the world, if only the rest of the world would listen. In fact, much of the rest of the world is looking at us in horror and dismay. The reality is that we do indeed have many wonderful things to offer the rest of the world. It's just that, well . . . we aren't God.

For such a powerful, wealthy, enlightened nation, we have some big problems. We have shame about them, too. When foreign dignitaries visit America, do we go out of our way to give them a tour of our slums? Do we point out cheerfully all of the local crack houses? Do we emphasize the tremendous and growing gap between rich and poor? We are ashamed, but we deny it. Denial is one of the most effective defenses against healthy or unhealthy shame.

During the spring 1992 riots in Los Angeles, CNN television interviewed people on the streets in European countries. The overwhelming response was, "We don't understand why you have so many guns in your country. It seems as if everybody has a gun!" Linda and I do some speaking in Canada now and then. The people there can't understand it either. Yet some of us in America actually make a connection between being a Christian and owning a gun, as if the two go together.

Between 1979 and 1987, handguns were involved in 9,200 murders, 12,000 rapes, 210,000 robberies and 407,600 assaults. On an average day, 10 children under age 18 are killed with handguns. Writing for the *New York Times,* Philip Hilts stated, "Gunshot wounds are the second leading cause of death among high-school age children in the U.S., and they are increasing faster than any other cause in that age group among both whites and blacks." He wrote that for black teenage males in major U.S. cities, gunshot wounds are the leading cause of death. He also noted that while people say they have guns to protect themselves from criminals, they actually kill themselves and family members 43 times more often than they shoot criminals. These statistics were compiled by the American Medical Association, not an antigun lobby. A *USA Today* cover piece noted that the National Rifle Association has 2.8 million members while Handgun Control, the nation's largest antigun lobby, has only 350,000 members. We just look the other way as our teenagers, black and white, die.

In truth, the world is shrinking. As it shrinks every country will be more exposed to the media, and with that exposure comes exposure of each country's shameful qualities. Overall, we are lucky to be Americans. We can look at poverty, alcoholism, riots or prejudice in other countries and pat ourselves on the backs for how well we are doing. Many people from other nations would, and do, give anything to live here. We must remember, however, that it is always easier to look at others and see their faults than it is to see our own. It was Jesus who said:

> Judge not, that you be not judged. For with what judgment you judge, you will be judged; and with the same measure you use, it will be measured back to you.
>
> And why do you look at the speck in your brother's eye, but do not consider the plank in your own eye? Or how can you say to your brother, "Let me remove the speck out of your eye;" and look, a plank is in your own eye?
>
> Hypocrite! First remove the plank from your own eye, and then you will see clearly to remove the speck out of your brother's eye.
>
> Matthew 7:1-6

In other words, let's keep helping other people and nations as much as we can, but let's not poke people in the eyes because we ourselves are blind. We need to ask ourselves some questions. Why are we so violent? Why are we so focused on *things,* as if things will make us whole? Why are we so afraid of sex and obsessed with sex at the same time, instead of letting it be a simple part of life? Why do we blame everyone else for our poverty instead of doing something about it? Our leaders from all major political parties and at all levels of government blame each other for the problem, but they are too scared to do anything to solve it. We elect our leaders. We need to tell them what we want.

Do we know what we want? Do we even want to know? It scares me to death when we shove our heads into the sand and deny that anything is wrong. It is this kind of cultural, system-wide denial that causes incest survivors to feel so crazy that they want to commit suicide. It is this same kind of denial that will cause an entire neighborhood, city or nation to feel so crazy that it wants to self-destruct. I love the country in which I live. I love my children, too. If I saw my children doing something to hurt themselves, like drinking alcoholically or using street drugs, I wouldn't bury my head in the sand and pretend it wasn't happening. My love for them would demand that I do something about it.

It's the same with America. If we call ourselves Christians, and if we claim to care for America and for the people who live here, then we have no choice but to say and do something about the shameful things we see. I'm not quite sure which to call it — ignorance, naivete, denial or all of the above — but we have become a nation of people who can't or don't want to think, learn, challenge or participate. That scares me a lot because when we are afraid, we become paralyzed. Then we start hurting each other again, just like we did 100,000 years ago when we met up in that valley.

Who Will Lead The Way?

With reason we ask, "But what can one person do?" The country is so big and the problems seem beyond repair. Despite all of our cultural and technological achievements, we are still human, and we are still in need of guidance from somewhere beyond ourselves. Where can we find some guidance? Who will lead the way? Will it be a talk-show host? A psychologist or psychiatrist? A seductive guru? Who will lead the way? How about a Neo-Nazi or a Ku Klux Klansman? We are lost and confused.

We need somebody to lead the way. Lead us! We'll follow! Just get going!

If it were only that simple. I may tell you that my beliefs are right and my leader is the best. You reply that your beliefs are right and your leader is the best. My religion is right and yours is wrong or vice versa. The world's Christians can't even agree on what Christianity means. What are we supposed to do?

When I get this confused, I always try to go back to the basic, and therefore, ultimate message. The more confused my clients become with all of the details and rules of their lives, the more I try to help them rediscover their basic, core issues. I try to make the issue as simple as possible for myself. The Scribes and Pharisees got so lost in the tangle of rules and regulations of their day that they completely lost sight of the reason for the rules.

Jesus dealt with that hypocrisy firmly, swiftly and unequivocally when He said, "Love your neighbor as yourself." I get the distinct impression that Jesus wasn't kidding around when He said this. It's such a simple, elegant summary of centuries of complicated theology that it leaves no room for argument or exception. He commanded us to love our neighbors as ourselves.

Of course, it still leaves room for interpretation by us flawed humans because we are never quite sure what anything means. Many Christian religions have articles or confessions of faith which are our attempts to define what Jesus meant. I encourage you to seek out the ones from your religion. Don't just read them. Really give some thought to what they are telling you.

I have reproduced below a segment of those articles from the Presbyterian Confession of 1967, since I currently belong to a Presbyterian church. I am not doing this to make you like or dislike this church. I am just doing it to give you an example:

> We believe that God's reconciliation of the human race creates one universal family. God breaks down every form of discrimination based on racial or ethnic difference. The Church as the community of reconciliation is called to cherish all people and to share life on every level, in work and play, in courtship, marriage and family, in Church and state. Congregations, individuals or groups of Christians who exclude, dominate, or disparage others, however subtly, resist the Spirit of God and repudiate the faith which they would profess.

That is a pretty unequivocal statement. Christ also said:

> Anyone who speaks a word against the Son of Man, it will be forgiven him; but whoever speaks against the Holy Spirit, it will not be forgiven him, either in this age or in the age to come.
>
> Matthew 12:32

If the Presbyterians are anywhere near right about their Confession of Faith, then I need to go back and look for the planks of prejudice in my own eye — in work and play, in courtship, marriage and family in Church and state. I have to look at how I exclude, dominate or disparage others, however subtly. That is a tall order. The good thing about a community statement like this is that it really helps me to understand what Christ has invited me to do. It means that I have some wise direction in my life. It means that I don't have to run around confused and lost all the time. But it also means that I have to make some tough choices. Believing in God or Jesus Christ does not mean that we get to quit thinking and just live by rote. If it were that simple, life would be frightening indeed.

Jesus always left the choices — our free will — up to us. So each time I am faced with a choice to live or not live by His Commandment, I must choose. Do I rent my apartment to a black man or not? Do I avoid, or condescendingly pity, a physically disabled person or not? Do I treat women like objects or not? Do I try to dominate and force my will and myself onto the woman or man in my life or not? Do I secretly rejoice when my children persecute gay people, or do I act as a Christian leader and require that my children ponder whether they are "doing unto others," while asking myself what I may have done to give them permission to become so cruel? Do I hang onto my fear of the unknown and my fear of differences so I can comfortably hate entire groups of human beings without having to struggle with the foreign? Or do I take the risk to keep learning and searching and wondering so I can inch my way out of the darkness and thereby teach my children to do the same?

Jesus' Commandment is a tall order. Thank goodness for His forgiveness. Thank goodness He knows how flawed and scared we are. Thank goodness that it's enough to keep trying to be better. Despite all the fear and hatred and prejudice and worry that we seem to carry around with us, if you look around there are always rays of hope.

Ignorance And Fear

Many theologians see ignorance, which is the foundation of fear, as the true cause of evil in the world. A child from a primitive culture is dying from appendicitis and the chief won't let the Western surgeon perform a routine operation to save his son's life. It seems so futile and pointless. The surgeon leaves the chief's land and mutters to himself, "This is evil." Amidst all of our wealth we have horrible poverty. We say, "This is evil." A priest sexually abuses an innocent young altar boy and we say, "This is evil." A parent batters an infant and we say, "This is evil."

In each case what I have described is actually the result of ignorance and fear. The chief is scared. Why should he trust a foreigner to cut open his son? He's never seen it done before. He has no history on which to rely.

What can we do about poverty? We care, but who can stop it? We elected the people we thought could help.

Right now we're too scared of poor people to be able to care. We need more jails to put them in because they're so angry and violent. Let's get the jails first so we can feel safe. Then we can worry about helping them to feel safe.

What about the priest? "Hang him!" we shout. I have a better idea. We already know why abuse by the clergy happens. We aren't ignorant. Let's just make sure that our religious institutions are accountable instead of blameless. Let's make sure that we have treatment programs for the tortured clergy. We know how to do that, too. Let's make sure that we don't let our own fear, ignorance and shame cause us to deny that the abuse is happening. That would really be evil.

The infant batterers? We know about the dynamics of that, too. It comes from being too stressed, from being abused themselves as children, from having shame about their normal human impulses, from not having parent education and healthy emotional choices. It all comes from fear and ignorance.

If it feels to you as if we have all gone to hell in a handbasket, stop and look around. This time don't turn off your television set. Instead watch it with a trained eye.

I was in the Los Angeles area when the riots broke out after the Rodney King verdict was handed down and I was glued to the TV like many others. What I vividly remember now is not so much the violence but the few stories that emerged during that crisis which were testaments to the goodness of the human spirit. I remember the group of African-American, Hispanic-American, Asian-American and Caucasian neighbors who banded together to protect the corner store owned by a peaceful Korean man "because it is our store, and he is our friend." That is an example of the communal force alive and well in America.

I saw African-Americans saving Caucasians from beatings by African-Americans. When it was all over, I saw

Hispanic Americans, African-Americans, Caucasians, Asian-Americans and everyone else pitching in and trying to help clean up the streets.

Don't Try To Save The Whole World: A Story Of Hope

Ignorance and fear. They are the cause of evil in the world. We all have ignorance and fear, but now and then one or two of us seem to be able to get beyond it just long enough to make a lasting difference. When that happens, it is because the people involved decided to deal with the life right in front of their noses instead of trying to fix the whole world.

I have a friend who is from Iran and who used to be a cab driver before he started his own business. He was raised in the Muslim religion. He fled to the United States to avoid the torment and upheaval in his homeland. I was touched by how much courage it must take to leave one's home and start over in another country. He had to learn English, which he had done pretty well. He had to take a job that was well below his educational level. He had to uproot his family.

As I came to know him and learn about his life and customs, I must admit that I felt some embarrassment about my own homeland and customs when compared to his. The warmth, family solidarity, humility and willingness to work that I saw in this man and his friends were striking. He has enriched my life by his example, without even knowing it.

He told me a wonderful story one day. He told it in a warm, good-natured way without bitterness, which also amazed me. He told of the rainy night he picked up a businessman in his taxi for what he thought would be a routine trip from the airport to the man's home. It wasn't routine. For the first half of the trip he had been making small talk with his customer as cab drivers are known to do. Suddenly the man lurched forward in his seat and demanded, "What country are you from?"

My friend answered, "Iran."

The man shouted, "You're a Muslim!"

My friend respectfully said, "Yes."

The man commanded, "Stop this cab right now! Let me out! I don't trust you! You Muslims are violent and crazy!"

My friend was worried for the man's safety, so he said, "It's raining, sir. I can't stop right here in the middle of the freeway and let you out. It would be too dangerous for you."

"I don't care! Let me out right now!"

"Sir," my friend pleaded in his new language, "It is not safe. I could not live with myself if I leave you on the side of freeway on a rainy night," but the man was adamant. My friend tried to give the man options. He said, "I can take you to your home or I can take you back to the airport, but I cannot drop you off on freeway."

The man said, "Let me out right now!"

Then my friend decided to try to get the man to think. He said, "I grow up in Iran. My father Muslim. He tell me to be Muslim, so I be Muslim. You grow up here. Your father tell you to be Christian, so you be Christian. What does it matter? I am a human being. I will not hurt you."

There was silence. My friend's heart was racing. He was scared, confused and even ashamed of his birthright, for no good reason. The man thought for an endless moment. He was scared, too. He was afraid that my friend was a wild, violent, murderous Muslim who would kill him, but the man curbed his fear long enough to listen to my friend's voice and to his reasoning. "This guy feels safe," the man said to himself. "As much as I hate to admit it, he has been more of a human being tonight than I have."

The man finally said, "Okay. Take me home."

Esquire Magazine ought to print this beautiful story of fear and conflict. It could be one of their cover stories entitled "Man At His Best." You see, there was nothing wrong with these two men. They were just like the two primitive men at the beginning of this book who met each other thousands of years ago in a valley and who were faced with the incredible survival decision to either cooperate or try to kill each other. We may transplant hearts and send women and men into outer space, but in many ways we are just like we have always been. We are still human.

There is a postscript to this story that is the final testament to the goodness of these two men. From that day forward the businessman, who had wanted to be dropped off on an interstate highway in the middle of a rainstorm rather than be driven home by what he thought was a murderous Muslim, always called my friend when he needed a taxi to or from the airport. These two men who were once terrified of each other became friends.

CHAPTER 11

Sin, Accountability And Forgiveness

I say to you that likewise there will be more joy in heaven over one sinner who repents than over ninety-nine just persons who need no repentance.
Luke 15:7

The Dilemma Of Alienation

Many people do not like the word "sin" because it conjures up images of wildly abusive, shaming religious beliefs and practices. Our clients who were raised Catholic back in the 1950s and 1960s share horror stories of being terrified into submission by sadistic, unhappy, rigid priests and nuns who railed at them about sin and evil. In most cases these kids were simply being kids and it was the adults who were "evil." Many children raised in Protestant denominations were terrified and shamed into focusing solely on their sins instead of being taught —

especially by example — how to be kind, loving, joyous Christians. Televangelists like to focus on our sins and our sinfulness because it is an easy way to manipulate people into giving large sums of money to such worthy causes as buying a new Mercedes limousine or an air-conditioned dog house.

Because of all the unhealthy, unproductive connotations of the word "sin," I prefer to talk about our mistakes, our errors and our isolation. It's the same thing, just different words that perhaps more people will be able to hear and respond to. In addition to this interpretation of "sin," philosophers and theologians also use the word "alienation." Wayne Oates wrote, "Sin as alienation from God and man is the composite and end result meaning of sin." In *The Denial of Death,* Ernest Becker pointed to an "astonishing historical merger of thought" between Rank and Kierkegaard in their conclusion that sin and neurosis were very much "the same thing — the complete isolation of the individual, his disharmony with the rest of nature, his hyperindividualism, his attempt to create his own world from within himself."

Becker went on to say that it is our human arrogance, grandiosity and unwillingness to admit our vulnerability that account for sin. When we get cut off from one another and from God, then we are in a state of "sin." This is the basic message from the story of Adam and Eve and the Fall. Christ spoke of it often. What we're really talking about, then, is that *when we sin, we are making a mistake that needs to be corrected in order to "return to a state of grace."* We have become cut off, isolated or alone in the world of God and humans, and therefore we need to do something to re-establish these relationships.

Mistakes and loneliness — these are what define "sin." In our work with adults who were hurt as children we find that loneliness and alienation are the most common symptoms. A man or woman comes into our office and begins to share with us, and it becomes clear right away that they feel as if they are the only ones on earth who have a problem. The shame and fear of "being found out" are overwhelming. Part of the healing of this alienation is to help people see that they are not alone — that we all have parts of ourselves that are painful or embarrassing. Jesus knew these hurts and fears that we all have and it was part of His mission to help us heal them.

He was so wise about this, too. Peter wanted to die and go up to heaven with Christ right on the spot, but Christ knew that we have to stay here and work things out with the rest of the human race. What a wonderful way to tell us gently that the path to holiness is through each other, here on earth, and not by some kind of exclusive relationship with God that is open to only a privileged few. When a reporter asked Mother Teresa about people calling her a living saint, she replied with humility:

> You have to be holy in your position, as you are. And I have to be holy in the position that God has put me. So it is nothing extraordinary to be holy. Holiness is not the luxury of the few. Holiness is a simple duty for you and for me. We have been created for that.

Yes, there is evil in the world. We make awful mistakes and then spend years trying to undo and untangle them. Even our churches do awful things — like accepting money as a way into heaven or creating the horrors of an Inquisition. The roots of sin or evil are ignorance and fear. Part of the alienation that our clients feel stems from their lack of knowledge of what other people are like inside. It is our job to help them realize they are not alone in their symptoms and pain. We all have these. We also have holiness. This is the paradox of being human that makes life challenging.

If we feel as if we are the only ones who have such evil flaws, how will we ever be able to heal? I tell myself, "No one has such awfulness inside of them as I do. Therefore, my only hope is to struggle with this awfulness alone. Maybe when I fix it, I will be able to rejoin the human race." So I struggle with my pain all by myself, never realizing that by doing it alone I am doing the one thing that will make sure I never heal. *The only solution to alienation from God and others is to reach out and start forming bonds with God and others.*

Because of the risks involved in reaching out to others, many people go halfway and simply reach out to God. They pray and pray all by themselves, convincing themselves that God is the only one who can be trusted. It's only halfway. Jesus said we have to stay here on earth and work it out among ourselves. He was right. Building a relationship with God is only half of the answer. The other half is to take the risk to find at least one other human being who will accept and love us. It would be nice to say that for each of us there is one person out there who will love us as Jesus did, but in reality that won't happen. Nobody out there is as perfect as Jesus.

That is the dilemma. I want the safety of Jesus' unconditional love, but He is in heaven and I am here on earth. He wants me to reach out to others and stop being alienated. I try now and then, but I keep getting hurt and withdrawing back into my shell. I don't know what to do.

As we work with our clients, they begin to trust that we are not going to hurt them. They struggle with the fact that we can't always be there for them. They get angry that we can't give them everything they didn't get as children, but they hang in there. A bridge between us starts to form. Then we ask them to take what they have learned about bridge-building in the safety of our office and go out into the world and build some more.

They go out and try. Excited about a new friend, they rush back to tell us about it. Days or weeks later they come in to tell us how the new friend hurt them or let them down. We feel their pain and then we help them to go back out and try again. They get angry at us for this. "I've been hurt enough!" Unfortunately there just isn't another answer for the problem. The only way to end alienation here on earth is to form bonds with other human beings. That's what Christ told us and that's what psychology tells us.

With time, the person begins to heal. With repeated attempts to reach out, and with the safety of the therapy relationship to fall back on, most people eventually learn how to build and maintain those bridges. A well-directed therapy group will hasten the process because a group of human beings has more healing power than just one therapist. Healing will happen if a therapist is skilled enough and healthy enough to care without sacrificing herself or himself in the process.

It's the same with good parenting or teaching, and it was what Jesus showed us by His actions. He cared for everyone, but He didn't compromise His principles or His stance toward life in the process. He was caring but firm, tolerant but clear about what He believed was right, and He was open to anyone who was willing to be open with Him. When people challenged Him hypocritically, He challenged them back with powerful humility.

Other "Sins:" Operating In The Extremes

If alienation and errors are "evil," then how do you know when you are making an error? How do you know whether or not the way you are behaving is good? How can you tell if you are being a permissive parent, a good parent or an authoritarian tyrant? When you express your feelings, how do you know whether you are over-reacting or under-reacting? Are there any general guidelines that can help us to know when we are making mistakes as opposed to acting in a healthy way?

Perhaps the best way to at least begin to get a handle on what is appropriate versus what is abusive is to imagine a continuum for the behavior you are thinking about. Then imagine the most extreme cases of that behavior. Usually this will help you to find what's healthy. Linda and I have learned over the years that when we or our clients are operating in the extremes, it is usually not good. As I go through the following examples, keep in mind that the goal is not to be boring and bland in your life. The goal is to avoid extreme positions that are destructive.

Black-And-White Thinking

The first and perhaps most destructive example of extremes being "evil" comes in the form of rigid, black-and-white thinking. This sort of thinking is characteristic of authoritarian or totalitarian despots, and it requires that we see the world in the way that a young, scared child might see it. As that kind of rigid thinking increases in a society, the kinds of evil that really angered Jesus Christ start to flourish.

Polarization — turning everything into opposites — is one of the more evil things that can happen in a society because it is so divisive. It brings out our fear and hatred instead of our desire to love and cooperate. Dynamic tension is important for a vibrant, spiritual life, but the kind of tension that results from rigid, black-and-white thinking is not often healthy. It usually leads to hatred, prejudice, intolerance, fear and society-wide abuse of human rights.

I hear some ultraconservative people saying things like, "all foreigners are bad," or "all people of color are bad," or "all homeless people are lazy." This is not only un-Christian, it is also illogical. Then I hear ultraliberals say or imply the opposite, that "all things foreign are good," or "all people of color are good," or "all homeless people are just victims of society." These extreme, polarized positions accomplish only one thing, and they accomplish it very well: They give us a reason to hate each other. This is why they are "sinful."

Some typical types of black-and-white thinking are shown below:

All clergy are good.	All clergy are bad.
All men are good.	All men are bad.
All foreigners are good.	All foreigners are bad.
Being conservative is always good.	Being liberal is always good.
Being quiet is good.	Being quiet is bad.
All people of color are good.	All people of color are bad.
It is good to be rich.	It is bad to be rich.

The list could go on and on, but I believe the message is clear. This kind of polarization breeds nothing but hatred and fear, which are the antitheses of Christianity.

Helping Others

At one end of this continuum would be those who spend no time at all helping others — they are completely caught up in their own lives and problems and have nothing to give to anyone else. At the other extreme would be those who have no time for themselves because they spend every waking minute helping others. Exhausted all the time, this person eventually gets sick or becomes abusive to others. Between these two extremes is a whole range of healthy combinations of "helping others" and "taking care of self."

For example, after five years of intense work with severely mentally ill patients, you might need to switch to a less emotionally demanding job so you can recharge your own batteries for a couple of years. If you don't, burnout may put you out of commission entirely. Or if you spend your entire working day in the service of others, you might choose to find your balance by spending evenings and weekends *not* in the service of others. Each person has a certain tolerance level for being around other people, and each person must respect that level or pay a price for not respecting it.

Anger

I referred to healthy versus unhealthy expressions of anger in earlier chapters. At one end of this continuum would be violent rageful anger. Most people would agree that this kind of anger is "evil" in the sense of being a mistake that alienates us from ourselves, each other and God. At the other end of the continuum would be the person who never expresses anger, even though we all feel it because we are all human. Actually, the anger is there — it just isn't expressed in a healthy way. It might come out sideways as nasty, hurtful, passive-aggressive sarcasm or teasing. Or it might come out indirectly as a withdrawal of love — the "silent treatment" or pouting, characteristic of a spoiled child but certainly not of a healthy adult. Many of our clients have said over the years they would rather have someone be overtly angry than covertly, passively angry like this because this hidden anger is so hard to live with.

Between these two painful "evil" extremes lies a whole range of healthy alternatives, from justifiable outrage to mild irritation or frustration. In other words, being healthy doesn't mean being boring. It just means trying not to damage ourselves or others as we go about our lives.

No Rules/All Rules

Permissive families with no rules are known to be damaging to children. Permissive work environments without any boundaries or limits are damaging to employees. Lack of rules and structure mean a lack of safety for everyone in the system. Some people create permissive systems because of their unhealthy guilt or pity. Others do so because they just don't care. Either way, the end result is the same. The system isn't good for anyone in it.

Rigid systems with too many rules are just as bad as permissive ones. Too many rules and restrictions indicate that the system is operating out of fear rather than out of responsible love. They strangle the life out of people in the system. We eventually become joyless and numb. Creativity stops. Problems don't get solved. Hatred and fear punctuate the day. The former Soviet Union will be in massive crisis for many years because of this kind of rigid rule.

And what of healthy rules? In healthy families, everyone has rules, routines and structure, but they also have freedom, openness and celebration. It takes quite a parent, manager or leader to create that kind of system because it isn't black and white. It is much easier to create a permissive or a rigid system because it doesn't take much thought or creativity to do it.

No Shame/All Shame

If a person has no shame, we say that they are "shameless." People who are shameless are grandiose, and they often dump their shame on everyone around them. Those who pronounce loudly that they "have no shame" are actually filled with it but are afraid to admit their vulnerability so they project it onto others. People who are shameless do shameful things.

People who are filled with shame but know it and express it aren't any better off. Shame has a purpose in letting us be human and accountable. To be filled with shame to the point of being emotionally paralyzed is not healthy. Healthy people can admit their limitations but also enjoy and be proud of their strengths and accomplishments. It is not bragging or grandiose to say, "I just did a good job, and I'm proud of myself."

No Closeness/Too Much Closeness

This is one of the most difficult "opposites" we struggle with. It relates to the struggle between agency and communion that I mentioned in an earlier chapter. This effort is what gives a good love relationship its life and breath and depth. It keeps relationships fresh. Either extreme can kill a relationship faster than just about anything.

Families or couples with no closeness are simply not in relationship. They may live under the same roof, share their genetics in the form of children and pay the same bills each month, but without closeness, families or couples are simply not families or couples. Most people can understand this type of pain. We have images of cold, lonely people separated by emotional gorges that rival the Grand Canyon, and we can feel the pain that others are experiencing in these relationships.

What about families or couples that are *too close?* Is this possible — that we could care too much and be too involved with each other? It is both possible and very damaging. Family systems theorists call this *enmeshment*. It appears in the form of a Dad or Mom who hovers over children, overprotecting and smothering. It comes in the form of children who are allowed to care too much about their parents' problems, when the parents should be worrying about their own problems so the children are free to be children.

In many families serious enmeshment is mistaken for devoted love. It never has the life-enhancing effects of real love. In an enmeshed family there are weak boundaries, whereas in a real love relationship there are clear, flexible boundaries. In an enmeshed family people carry the burden of each other's feelings. With healthy love, people care about each other without overwhelming or being overwhelmed by feelings.

We once consulted with a group of family physicians who were concerned about the health of a child and wondered if it could be "psychological." In the first session with the family it was clear that the child was terribly enmeshed — symbiotically connected — to his mother, and was unable to separate and begin to grow up. When we told this to the physicians, one of them was outraged that we were implying that a family could "love" too much. Despite this doctor's protests, the family got help. The symbiosis was very painfully broken and the little boy was able to grow up — as was his mother.

No Internal Limits/All Internal Limits

This is actually a variation of and a by-product of the "no rules/all rules" extremes mentioned above. One way to learn to have no internal limits is to grow up with no rules, limits or boundaries from the outside — from your parents. I have it as a separate section here because it lets us see that boundaries are inside of us and that we have choices about our internal boundaries once we become adults.

For example, if I can't seem to stop myself from saying destructive or embarrassing things to others as I "shoot from the hip," then I have a problem with weak internal boundaries. If I am impulsive rather than responsibly spontaneous, I will do all kinds of things that I later regret but I won't seem to be able to stop myself.

If my internal boundaries are rigid, I will be compulsive and rigidly overcontrolled. I will be afraid to take risks. I will have a lot of unhealthy guilt that keeps me paralyzed when I need to act. There are times when it is healthy and constructive to have strong internal boundaries, and there are times when it is much better to loosen up on those limits. People with flexible internal limits can adjust to life's changing demands because they aren't stuck in either extreme.

Before you move on to the next section, I urge you to reflect on the polar opposites you just read. I truly believe that much of the "sin," "evil," and alienation in the world can be traced to operating in the extremes.

Accountability

Once you have identified that you have made a mistake, then the next step is to let yourself be accountable for it. Through this process, people can begin to heal their isolation, alienation, shame and errors. Building bridges is very important but part of this healing process includes taking stock of the bridges we've wrecked. A woman may have been abused as a child and therefore she abuses her own children until she gets help to lead her out of the darkness of her abusiveness. She also needs to take responsibility for what she has done to date.

Accountability means that we admit our errors and tell the people we have hurt that we know we have hurt them. It also means that we do whatever it takes to stop the hurting. A man who tells his wife he is sorry he makes fun of her all the time, but who doesn't do anything to correct his own inner pain that causes him to abuse her, is not being accountable. Just saying "I'm sorry" is the oldest con in the world. We have to change quite a bit before others will feel safe enough to rebuild a bridge with us.

I caution people when they are first trying to be accountable. It is easy to hurt others further in the process of working toward forgiveness. If it finally comes to my attention that I had hurt one of my children when I yelled at her loudly, then I need to sit down with her and say, "When I yelled at you, I could see that it scared you. I'm sorry that I scared you."

Do you see how simple it is? Any other verbiage such as excuses, rationales, justifications or explanations would be further abuse. Can you see why? It is because the bridge that must be healed is simple. It doesn't matter if I was tired and cranky. It doesn't matter if I had a bad day. It doesn't matter if I didn't mean to yell. I yelled, she was scared and that is that. Of course, it would be severe abuse if I said, "Well, I'm sorry that I yelled at you, but I didn't mean to, and anyway, it wasn't that loud. You shouldn't be so sensitive. You've always been the sensitive one in the family." If you can't see why this is severe abuse, please get some help to see it.

Are We Accountable For Everything?

If I call you at 9:00 P.M. and proceed to pour out my life's problems to you several nights a week, and it is obvious that I am not willing to get other kinds of help, what would you do? I hope that you would tell me firmly and tactfully that you won't be taking these kinds of calls from me anymore, that you are open to a more limited kind of relationship, but you are not willing to be my crisis counselor. I have had to say that to a former friend or two, and I always felt some hefty guilt afterwards. Should I act on that guilt and apologize to you for hurting your feelings or should I just let it go? Right. I should just let it go.

We are not responsible and accountable for all of the feelings that people have. We are certainly not required to mollycoddle others. If you have a child who is rude and obnoxious, and you let that child be rude and obnoxious to me, then I will let both you and your child know that I am angry and want the intrusiveness to stop. In these cases it is the other person who needs to experience their shame and become accountable. You need to be a better parent to your child. Even if you don't want to be, you at least have the obligation to keep him from harming others. In the case of the 9:00 P.M. phone calls, it is *my* problem if I feel shame when you tell me to stop calling you in crisis. It is *I* who need to make changes and be accountable.

Must I Do Something To Be Accountable?

It may be enough simply to say something, but only if the offensive behavior has stopped. The first thing that must happen is that the damaging behavior stop immediately.

Saying, "I'm sorry," and then doing it some more tomorrow is hypocrisy. Even if the offensive behavior stopped years ago, an apology and an accounting may not be enough. It just depends on how deep the damage is.

If you started sexually abusing your infant 30 years ago and the abuse stopped 25 years ago, an accounting and apology may be enough. You may also need to take responsibility for the extensive therapy bills that your child may require to heal from the incest. You may need to attend some of those therapy sessions and allow your apologies to be witnessed by your child's family and therapist. We see more and more parents coming forward and accepting these responsibilities, which is very encouraging.

Healing our "sins," correcting our mistakes and errors, rebuilding the broken bridges between us, being accountable — they are all pretty much in the same ballpark. There is nothing worse than being hurt or betrayed by a fellow human being, but there are few things more spiritual and powerful than being part of an honest amends process between two people. One of the most rewarding experiences that I have as a therapist is when parents and children come in and do this process. It is simply wonderful to see an old man cry and apologize to his grown son about something that happened 30 years ago, and then to see the son cry and accept his dad's apology. It puts life in a whole different light whenever it happens. It is surely the antithesis of evil.

Steps To Accountability

Please realize that only you can judge whether you are being accountable. Also, false pride and ego are the biggest impediments to bridge-building between people. If you believe you don't have to own up to your abusiveness because, by God, you are the man and the head of the household and your children must honor you no matter what — think again. You are being "evil." You are passing the sins of the father to his children. Deep down inside, you know it. I know you do because you are a human being, and we all operate alike. So swallow your false pride. Be a leader. Change the abusive rules in the family system. I challenge you to show some of the courage that Jesus Christ showed. Go ahead. Heal your relationship with your kids or your wife. It doesn't mean you're a wimp. To make it clearer I have listed below the steps required for accountability in many situations.

STEPS TO ACCOUNTABILITY

1. I become aware that I have done something that has hurt someone.
2. I think, feel and even get outside opinions about my responsibility for that hurt.
3. I make sure that I am able to stop the offensive behavior. If I am unable, then I immediately seek professional help. I don't wait to see "if things will get better by themselves."
4. Once the offensive behavior has stopped, then I tell the person that I did what I did. I say I am sorry that I hurt the other person by what I did. No excuses here, no weaseling out of responsibility and absolutely no blaming of the victim.
5. I hope for forgiveness from the other person, but I know this is a separate issue. I cannot make another person forgive me. I must wait patiently, as Christ taught us to do. It would be more abuse for me to chase you around, begging for forgiveness.

Forgiveness

How can we forgive a person who is still hurting us? In one sense we can't. We can turn the other cheek, we can struggle to see the goodness in the other person, we can understand why they are doing it and we can pray for them, but what I mean here by forgiveness also includes our own dignity and safety. It means restoring the relationship bridge between ourselves and this person. If they keep breaking the bridge, then how can they have a relationship with them? Bear with me as I develop this point before jumping to conclusions. I don't think what I am saying here is in disagreement with Christ's teachings.

A man I know was emotionally damaged by his mother. When he was a teenager, she would go up to him and run her fingers through the hair on his chest and say, "Oh, you're really looking like a man now!" When he came home from a date, she would be waiting up for him no matter how late it was so she could "chat" with him. She'd ask him details of his date, what he and the girl did, how it made him feel and so on. Clearly this woman was covertly sexually abusing her son.

The man had painful relationship problems as an adult. He was angry with women but easily seduced by them. He was in therapy with me to work on these issues. It took many months before he was able to uncover the hidden sexual abuse that he had suffered. It took many months more before he could work through his shame and outrage, but he did. Then it was time to deal with his mother. She was still treating him more like a husband/lover than a son, so my client decided that before he could let go of his fear and anger toward her, he would have to get her to stop. That made a lot of sense to me.

The problem was Mom wasn't having any part of it. He very gently tried to tell her that she needed to talk to him differently because he wasn't her husband, he was her son. She just dug in her heels and told him he was crazy and that his therapist was crazy. Her shame and false pride were really working overtime. What was my client to do? He didn't want to be abused anymore, and he had tried respectfully to get Mom to stop the abuse. She left him only one alternative — he had to cut way back on the amount of contact he had with her. He felt guilty at first, but he realized that it was Mom who was not being accountable. She was not allowing a bridge to build between them. She kept tearing down the bridge with her ongoing abuse.

Now that he was safe, he could at last forgive Mom. He was sad that her own "sin" — pain, alienation, errors — inside of her would not let her grow up and he hoped that she would change. He wished her the best. He had forgiven her. She never changed but he did. By working through the "evil" that he had grown up with and that was inside of him, he learned to have healthy relationships with other adults instead of using his own children as partners, pals and a built-in social support system. The sins of his father and mother — the covert emotional incest that had hurt him — did not have to be visited on his children. That is what forgiveness is about.

CHAPTER 12

Embracing The Many Faces Of Prayer

But when you pray, do not use vain repetitions as the heathen do. For they think that they will be heard for their many words.

Matthew 6:7

When Christ gave His followers The Lord's Prayer, He was doing much more than giving people something to be repeated mindlessly by rote. He was teaching them something. In today's language, He was saying, "You're getting lost in all of the rituals and compulsiveness that you've been practicing. You're losing the meaning of prayer." Perhaps most important of all, He was saying, "Keep it simple."

A recent cover story in *Newsweek* was titled, "Talking To God: An Intimate Look At The Way We Pray." In the article the authors cited some of Father Andrew Greeley's research which indicated that 78% of Americans pray at least once a week, 57% once a day — and that 20% of atheists and agnostics report praying once a day. In that same article the authors cited a statistic from Poloma and Gallup which indicates that when we pray, 42% of us ask for material things. There's the rub. Is that what prayer is really about? Is it that specific? If I ask for a new house, will I get it? If I ask to get into Harvard University, will I get in?

What's The Point Of The Lord's Prayer?

Jesus realized that the people of His time were "getting out of whack" with their praying — that rituals were becoming more important than meanings. One day He gave us an elegant prayer that was meant by Him to be an *example* of how to pray. He more or less said, "Pray *like* this."

Because every Christian child must memorize The Lord's Prayer early in life we sometimes forget it's not supposed to be mindlessly recited over and over so we can earn more "credits" to get into heaven. That attitude is a misunderstanding of what Jesus was trying to teach us by the example of His prayer.

Let's take a look and see what it's all about, keeping in mind that these are simply my thoughts about the prayer. Yours may be different.

Our Father Who Art In Heaven, Hallowed Be Thy Name

This is pretty straightforward. It simply means that you believe there is a Creator in the universe — a Prime Mover — and that there is a spiritual world beyond the physical world we know through our five senses. You acknowledge that this Being is holy, spiritual and sacred.

Thy Kingdom Come, Thy Will Be Done, On Earth As It Is In Heaven

When you say this, you are saying there is some kind of overall plan for the universe that your Creator knows about and that you want to live your life according to that plan. The part that says "Thy will be done" has been cause for centuries of debate about free will, for obvious reasons. If God's will is going to be done, then what responsibility do I have for my life? If I have free will, then what chance do I have of doing the right thing when I'm not even sure of what God's will is? I find that, intuitively, this statement makes sense to me and to a lot of other people.

I like to interpret it this way. I'm here, living my life. There's a plan for me but not in the sense of a rigid script. I can choose different paths at choice points along the way. There are probably more paths than just one which will lead me to where I am ultimately supposed to go. If I stay open to the energy in the universe, to God, then I will get some help along the way in making those "path-choices." When I say, "Thy will be done," I am saying that I am not God. I do not have all the answers, I am continually growing and maturing and I want some help and direction now and then because I don't have all the answers. It's really quite simple to understand. Healthy parents and children operate this way all the time.

Give Us This Day Our Daily Bread

I really don't think this is too hard either. "Daily bread" means the ability to survive on the planet. It doesn't necessarily mean to survive on the planet with more bread, fields, wagons, buildings or jewels than everyone else. It is a simple request that we have enough. I find that the most spiritual people I know don't pray for specific things, especially not for material things. They pray quietly, in the way that they live and experience the world, for a heightened connection with themselves, each other and the universe. I think this is also what "daily bread" means — emotional food as well as physical.

And Forgive Us Our Trespasses As We Forgive Those Who Trespass Against Us

Forgiveness of error, whether intentional or not, is one of the distinguishing characteristics of exceptional human beings. In this part of the prayer Christ put us in an interesting double bind of sorts because we are not always that ready to forgive people who have hurt us. By asking God to forgive us as we forgive others, it presumes that we are forgiving others. This is a direct challenge to our notions of fairness and equality. "Yes," we say. "I guess that's fair. It would be hypocritical to ask God to forgive us if we are not willing to forgive each other." I am constantly impressed by how Christ always challenged us to think.

Does forgiveness mean that we should continue to keep up a relationship with a man or woman who is abusing us? I don't think so. Forgiveness does not require that we remain victims of ongoing abuse. As I said earlier, I believe that true forgiveness can only come after we are safely away from the abuser. Remember that being human is also about survival and dignity. It's not about collaboration with abuse. To collaborate with someone's abuse by allowing it to continue when there is a way to stop or avoid it is not holy. In fact, it is degrading to abusers to allow them to continue abusing. It robs abusers of their dignity and it robs victims of theirs. When there is no way to get away from the abuser, then the only solution is to surrender until a way opens up.

Christ was clear. We are meant to forgive each other our mistakes and errors as best we can. We are meant to rely on His example for that forgiveness as best we can. That is a very tall order, one that challenges all of us every day until the day we die.

Lead Us Not Into Temptation, But Deliver Us From Evil

Here we ask that God help us to stay on a healthy path, even though we must recognize that temptation and error are part of the human condition. With this statement we recognize that we have feelings, urges, drives and emotions which can lead to behavior that can hurt us or others. We can cross over the mountain into the next valley and kill all of the people there because our children are dying of starvation. Or we can try a different approach, in which your clan and my clan cooperate and share our resources so all of our children can survive. The temptation simply to take what we need despite the consequences will be strong. Cooperation will only work if both clans agree to work together. Evil and temptation are part of survival. In other words, Christ was trying to get us to think about our mistakes before we make them.

If "evil" and "sin" are just ways to say "alienation," "mistakes or errors" or "fear and ignorance," then what we are asking for in this part of the prayer is help to change. We want to be aware of our mistakes, be as accountable as we are able, forgive as best we can, keep coming out of the darkness of ignorance by being open to new knowledge, try not to act impulsively out of raw fear, and keep taking the risks to build bridges with other human beings and with our Creator.

For Thine Is The Kingdom, The Power And The Glory Forever

This statement is about the timelessness or eternity of God, about God's infinite power and about the infinite joy of being connected to God. It means there is something out there that transcends us, the physical world, our bodies and our limited human perceptions. By all the preceding parts of The Lord's Prayer, Christ was telling people they could share in that. God is not an angry vengeful Being. By stating how much power and glory is God's, the prayer also requires that we have humility and admit we are not all-powerful ourselves. This is actually comforting to most people. After all, would you want to have responsibility for the conduct of the entire universe?

It's easy to see how this works if you look at children and power. Children don't do well when they are allowed to have unbridled freedom and power. They don't do well when they are rigidly restrained either. They seem to do best when someone is in charge. That person in charge must be kind, open, trustworthy and yet also willing to set limits for the child. Under those conditions children feel safe and they are able to grow up to fulfill their potential without becoming self-destructive in the process. "It's Your universe," we say to God. "I'll do my best with it, but I'll be needing your help."

I apologize to those of you who are theologians or who have studied The Lord's Prayer for years and have uncovered all of its nuances and subtleties. My intention was not to do the definitive interpretation of this prayer. My intention was to highlight how simple a prayer it is. It demonstrates how important it is for us, as we pray or meditate, to keep it simple and on track. I believe Christ was trying to tell us that when He gave us The Lord's Prayer. I also believe He was teaching us how to pray, rather than expecting us to just repeat what He said. He was very critical of that kind of rote mimicking.

The Many Faces Of Prayer

If spirituality is related to how we think, feel and act, as I noted in an earlier chapter, then it follows that prayer must be related to these three basic human activities as well. People who define prayer only as recitation of standards, such as The Lord's Prayer or Now I Lay Me Down To Sleep, are missing the point of Christ's message. He was trying to teach us by His actions, His feelings and His thoughts that prayer is much more than this.

I believe prayer is an openness and a willingness and an attitude. It can be reverent and solemn or it can be joyous and exuberant. It can come from a place of loneliness, sadness, fear and despair. It can be a connectedness with all of the pain in the world, or with all of the creativity in the world or with all of the awe and wonder in the world. It can be a heightened awareness and connection with one's Creator at a conscious level or it can be the same heightened awareness at an unconscious level. Sometimes our most powerful prayers are the actions we take each day that are consistent with our Christian beliefs. In other words, for some people life is simply a prayer.

Thinking Prayer

Sometimes prayer is cognitive. When we are thinking and wrestling with a personal problem, for example, we may be praying and not even be aware of it. When we ask God directly for an answer or a sign that will help us figure something out, we are praying. I believe theologians, astrophysicists, philosophers, biologists and anthropologists are all praying in a cognitive way because, as they strive to know more about the universe, they are sharing more fully and deeply in creation. As children many of us fantasized what it would be like when we died and went to heaven, where we would become "more like God" and would therefore have the answers to all of the mysteries of the universe. Knowledge is one of the things that makes human beings more evolved than lower animals. It is one of the things that brings us closer to the universe, closer to creation and closer to God.

The Bible is literally riddled with references to *Light* and *Dark*. Out of the darkness was the universe created. Those who believe will come into eternal life and eternal light. Darkness implies not only evil in the old "fire and brimstone" sense of the word, but also ignorance. The more we live in intellectual darkness, the more we will live like those primitive peoples who first inhabited the earth thousands of years ago. With our primitive and barbaric customs and beliefs, we will kill each other and torture each other and then use irrational fears or beliefs to justify our decisions to act this way. People who don't think, leave themselves open to manipulation and seduction. People who don't think can easily be tricked into doing all kinds of "evil" things, like hating their neighbors because of their skin color, race or beliefs. They can even be tricked into committing mass suicide, as were the followers of Jim Jones.

Prayer definitely has something to do with thinking. We talk about using our God-given talents. Using our brains is one way to do that. When you are reciting a prayer that you already know, and you think and reflect upon its meaning, you are praying. When you struggle with the meaning of life, when you wonder whether or not there is a God, when you question established dogma or teachings of your church, government or school, you are praying. When you find one small piece of the puzzle in the search for a cure for cancer or AIDS, when you memorize all the bones and muscles of the human body for your anatomy class, when you discover a new prime number, when you figure out how to do fractions, you are also discovering something wonderful about the universe. You are becoming more like God, and you are praying.

If all you ever do is think, then I believe your life and perhaps even your prayer is out of balance. I'll leave the final judgment about that up to your Creator, but I have a hunch I may be on to something here. If you don't think at all, then I suspect you're out of balance in your prayer as well.

Feeling Prayer

Not all of us are destined to become astrophysicists or molecular biologists. Even if we are, we're missing two-thirds of the boat if all we ever do is think. Prayer is also about our feelings and our connectedness with the emotional part of creation. In fact, it is through our feelings that we experience what might be called spiritual ecstasy — that feeling I described in the earlier chapter on spirituality. John MacMurray argued this strongly in *Reason And Emotion.*

Theologian Friedrich Schleiermacher made healthy dependency and emotional intimacy a central feature of his concept of God. The notion of being able to depend on God is one of the most appealing ones I have encountered in my intellectual travels through theology. Dependency is tied in so intimately with shame, and our need to depend on our parents is so powerful, that the idea that God is The Ultimate Being Upon Whom We Can Depend makes a tremendous amount of emotional sense to many of us. Being able to depend on someone, especially when we really need help, often produces a warm safe feeling. Shame is a feeling which in its healthy form allows us to feel grateful and humble.

Some religions or congregations flatly discourage feelings, relegating them to the back burner of spiritual experience. Other religions or congregations say that feelings are important but create rituals so numbing and boring and repetitive that people in the congregation are dissociated and "gone" throughout the entire service or ceremony. Some religions or congregations emphasize feelings too much. People in an "over-feeling congregation" have lots of fervent emotional moments, but they are easily led astray and are easily worked into a frenzy of irrational, destructive, un-Christian behavior. It is important to feel and think.

Feeling prayer is important. We are emotional beings. The way that we have our deepest intimacy with others is via our emotions. To put our emotions in the back seat doesn't make sense to us, especially when we view prayer as a way to have a relationship with our Creator. So go ahead, let yourself feel supported by God. Let yourself get angry at God for not bailing you out or for the tragedy that just happened to you. Be sad with God and hope that things will work out. Trust in God, but don't give up your will to fight your own fights. Rejoice and be thankful in the presence of God, and let that joyful noise ring up to the heavens. Share your pain with God. Share your fear with God and ask God to help you deal with your fear. These are all feelings. As you have a conversation with your Creator, let there be some feelings there. They're there anyway. Simply let yourself know that they are.

Action Prayer

One might say that Mother Teresa's life is a prayer. Certainly, Jesus' life was a prayer. It makes sense because who we are is more than what we think and feel. Otherwise you or I could be saints and psychopathic liars at the same time. Our actions are important. Christ was very firm about this. He spoke of how we treated one another, not just what we felt about one another. He spoke of "doing unto others." The hypocrisy that made Him so upset was characterized by people who did things that were inconsistent with what they professed to believe.

What we do is as important as what we think and feel. All you have to do is ask yourself who is "holier" in the following situation: a person who treats others with fairness and kindness, but who consciously prays to God once a week, or a person who treats others like scum, but who consciously prays every day? I don't believe the "action" part of prayer has to be some kind of great work that gets recognized by society either. Nor did Jesus. False holiness and public prayer "to look good" so offended Him that He admonished people to pray alone, silently, so as not to call public attention to themselves or their prayers.

Our action prayers can be like those of The Good Samaritan — going out of our way to help someone simply because there is another human being in need. If God is, indeed, the ultimate one upon whom we can depend, then to let others depend on us now and then is surely a form of prayer and simple holiness, as Mother Teresa noted. It is a form of "being like Jesus Christ," as He wished we would be.

Meditative Prayer

Marcus Borg emphasized the deeper form of prayer that Jesus and other mystics engaged in, during which one becomes silent and alone and thereby is able to become much closer to God. We use the word "meditation" to describe this activity, but if practiced the way Christ did it, it is much more than simple meditation. It is, as Borg said, an opportunity to sit "quietly in the presence of God." This form of prayer takes time, of course, which is a commodity that escapes many of us, but it is an activity that we sorely need to try.

Be Open To Connections With Something Beyond Yourself

Prayer is all of these things. It is an openness. It is a posture. It is a willingness. It is a longing. It is a hope and a dream. It is an action, a thought and a feeling. Most of all, prayer is a willingness to be connected with something beyond ourselves. Whether or not you believe in an afterlife, you can still be prayerful. Whether or not you believe you will be rewarded in the hereafter, you still have the obligation to live a good life if you are a human being. I believe this is a need that we all have.

Lynda Winter, a colleague of ours in Dayton, Ohio, who endured an excruciating year of chemotherapy for cancer recently, came to grips with the question of an afterlife during those agonizing months. She told us that, regardless of what was to happen to her after she died, she realized it was important to live a life now that she could deeply perceive as *enough.* In no uncertain terms, "enough" meant much more to her than material possessions. It meant having an impact on the world in ways that were possible for her. It meant being honest and kind, trying to heal her own wounds and therefore help others to heal theirs. It meant being the best parent possible. It meant being a loving partner and friend.

Research on aging also gives us some clear direction here. Erik Erikson's last stage of adult development — Integrity versus Despair — is resolved in the positive direction of integrity, wholeness and peace when people take the risks to continue growing, learning and being accountable right up until the end. People who continue to risk growing find that death is not frightening. They experience the so-called "ravages" of old age to be simply the next challenge with which to struggle and from which to grow. Having faced all of the earlier challenges of human development, this last challenge is much easier to face because they have a long history of growing.

On the other hand, people who have remained closed off and defended against the challenges and mysteries of life tend to interpret old age and death as powerful enemies that will ultimately ruin what little peace they may still have. The classic research conducted by Bernice Neugarten and her colleagues bore this out. They concluded that people who faced their life crises head on, all the way through life, adjusted to old age and death just fine. The work of Elisabeth Kubler-Ross on death and dying, as well as work by many others, also supports this idea. That is why it is so important to find the goodness and meaning in life regardless of one's religious beliefs. That is why it is so important to become connected with something beyond ourselves. That is what human spirituality is all about. Spirituality requires relationship. So does prayer.

Whether your prayer is in the form of questioning and searching for meaning or whether it is manifested in your good works or your emotional response to your fellow humans, a loving God or the Universe, let your prayers flow. And as Jesus Christ taught us long ago, don't pray so that others think you are wonderful. Pray from a stance of humility and wonder. That kind of surrender is safe. The paradox is that when we surrender in that way, we become more powerful in ways that will pay off for us and those around us right up until the day we die.

Structured Prayer

While all of the things mentioned above can be part of one's praying, I personally find that a few structured prayers are important and helpful as long as they don't become meaninglessly rote. The prayer below is one I put together for myself from many religious influences I have found meaningful. It is derived from *The Apostles' Creed, The Irish Blessing, Christ's Great Commandments* and *Step 11 Of Alcoholics Anonymous.* It means a lot to me and helps me focus on what I find particularly important in life, which I think is an essential part of prayer.

> God, the Father almighty, Creator of heaven and earth: Please hold us in the palm of Your hand, carry us into Your kingdom and give us peace.
>
> God, the Son, Christ my Brother and Savior: Please help me to love my neighbor and myself for the love of You.
>
> God, the Holy Spirit, giver of wisdom and grace: Please breathe Your life into my soul, so that I might have knowledge of Your will for me and the power to carry that out.
>
> Amen

CHAPTER 13

Dare To Be A Christian With Your Mind, Heart And Feet

For I have given you an example, that you should do as I have done.
John 13:15

How We Teach And Learn: A Review

I have worked with human beings most of my adult life as a parent, a teacher and a psychologist. I know the truth behind the maxim that children learn what we do, not what we say. Adults also learn what we do, not what we say.

For example, as a psychologist I am concerned with helping my clients learn to set boundaries. Healthy people can set limits on themselves and can also protect themselves from the intrusions of others when need be. At first, like all inexperienced parents, teachers and psychologists, I just tried to tell my clients that they needed to have clear boundaries. They would leave the therapy session with renewed resolve to protect their privacy from nosy neighbors or pushy salespeople or abusive relatives, but they would get into crises over their lack of boundaries. Then they would return with stories of failure.

I would tell them how to set the boundaries again, but this time I would tell them that if they got into a personal crisis, they should call me almost anytime, day or night, and we would nip it in the bud together. As the client left, I would give them a business card with my home telephone number written on it. The client would feel wonderful and warm and supported. I would feel useful, needed and very caring. Then the client would call that afternoon or evening in crisis over another failure to set boundaries and we would process it on the telephone for a good long time.

You probably have figured out the ending and the moral to this story already. By my words, I was teaching my client about boundaries. By my actions, I was teaching my client to be totally without boundaries. I believe that I confused many a client by this inappropriate behavior. If you are one of them, I hereby apologize to you.

What I do nowadays is assume that my clients can handle their crises during the week. I also assume they need to know that I have boundaries, which for almost all of them includes not calling me at home, on weekends or while I am on vacation. There are exceptions, of course, as in the case of a life-threatening emergency. It is my responsibility to help my clients learn quickly the difference between a daily crisis and a life-threatening emergency.

You may think this is harsh on my part. I certainly felt that way when my therapist showed that he had clear boundaries with me. I was hurt, angry, embarrassed and angry, hurt and embarrassed again. Yet I will be forever grateful for his boundary-setting. As he gently but very firmly refused to let me manipulate him or grow overly dependent on him, he was teaching me by his behavior that it is okay to set boundaries.

After months of struggling with my own and my therapist's boundaries, I was blessed with a painful opportunity to try to set an important boundary with someone very close to me. As I struggled inside with how I might hurt that person, how they might abandon me and how guilty I would feel after setting the boundary, I reached inside of myself and found a message or "tape" from my therapist's *behavior.* My therapist had set very clear boundaries with me and I hadn't died, I hadn't lost my respect for him or myself and I was still okay. All of a sudden I found the strength and courage to tell this loved one what I needed to tell them. I was able to follow through with keeping the boundary.

In a small but significant way I began to feel safer and more effective in the world. My dignity began to increase. I didn't have to feel as angry. I didn't have to feel like such a victim. The other person and I continued to have a relationship, too, but it was a new relationship because I had set the boundary and stuck with it. It was an amazingly elegant process. So simple, yet so hard. I know that I was successful because I had learned it from the actions of my therapist in his dealings with me. I had learned it because I chose to stay with this therapist rather than running away in anger and shame.

A great teacher, parent or therapist knows that the best way to help someone learn a new way of doing things is to demonstrate the new behavior. That is why Christ was such a great teacher. He taught not just with words, but also by His behavior. I believe that many people today have lost the basic message of Christianity because they have forgotten this simple truth.

The Role Of Rules

Rules and regulations are important so that people have some guidelines for how to live, especially when they are under stress. Sometimes you might feel angry enough to shoot someone. It is only the rule against killing that keeps you from being controlled by those dangerous impulses of the moment. Later you are thankful for the rule because without it, you might have done something you would regret for the rest of your life.

Rules, laws and regulations are a necessary and important part of life. Most of us know this, but sometimes we get lost in the maze of rules and regulations by which we all must live.

Many rules are important for our survival. When we were children, our parents told us not to ride our bikes at night without a light or reflective material on our clothing. This is a good rule. They told us to eat good food and to brush our teeth. Those are good rules. You should keep your seat belt on when you aren't walking around the airplane during a flight. You should exercise regularly. You should not play with a loaded gun. These are good rules, too.

Rules are there to help us live safely and in harmony with one another. Like anything else, too much of a good thing isn't very good. I believe this was one of the most important messages Christ gave us by His teaching and by His example. When He arrived on the scene, many of the religious leaders of His time were compulsive rule-followers who had lost their spirituality, their respect for human life and their ability to teach effectively. Many of them were hypocritical. They spent hours arguing about rules and regulations while the humanity around them suffered indignity, torture, slavery and death. They had little compassion. They were fakes.

This hypocrisy angered and offended Christ, and in no uncertain terms He moved to set the record straight. Most theologians will agree that one of the major messages of Christianity is: We must not get so caught up in miniscule rules and regulations we forget the overall purpose behind the rules.

Christ said, "Do unto others as you would have them do unto you." Of course He didn't just say this. He lived it and practiced it and challenged others with it by the way He lived. In today's vernacular He said, "You people are getting lost in all these rules. You say you are holy, then you turn around and shame others and believe that you are better than everyone else. You have no shame. You deny your humanity and therefore you deny your holiness. You are abusing one another in God's name. You need to stop focusing on the little rules and bring back into focus the One Big Rule. Stop hurting each other in the name of God and in the name of rules!"

To some this is very confusing. He says, "Don't follow the rules," and then He gives us some other rules to follow. What are we to do? In His short lifetime Christ broke rules all over the place and got into trouble for it, but it wasn't a random, thoughtless, destructive breaking of rules. He broke rules that were destructive so there would be new room opened up for a better rule. In the end He died because he scared people with His behavior, His beliefs and His feelings about those destructive rules and practices.

A good teacher knows that some rules are necessary for decent living. A good teacher also knows that each human being is decent inside. Provided the right environment, that goodness will come out and shine. The trick is to provide enough direction so people feel safe, along with enough freedom so people can develop their unique talents. You might try to make everyone in your class become a nuclear physicist, but that would be "evil." It would only be fair to the one or two kids who are meant to be nuclear physicists by their unique blend of ability and interest.

Who Will Be Our Role Models?

A portion of this book has focused on what's wrong with the way many of us practice our Christianity, yet when I take the time to look around, I see plenty of goodness, values and consistency in people. I see it in the Iranian taxi driver who patiently shared his background with the businessman. I see it in the businessman who overcame his irrational fear of Muslims when he rode home with the Iranian taxi driver. I see it in the African-American family who risked their lives to hide a gunshot-wounded white journalist from the murderous mobs during the Los Angeles riots. I see it in the Christian mother who went on the ABC news program *20/20* and courageously admitted that she had been wrong in covertly shaming and isolating her gay son "in the name of religion." She said his suicide could perhaps have been avoided, that she was sorry and that she had been misdirected by her religion on the issue of how to respond to a son who was gay. I see it in Mother Teresa. I see it in the great theologian Karl Rahner, who spent his entire adult life ministering to his parishioners, personally responding to all of his mail from all over the world and remaining a humble priest, while writing his theological works "in his spare time."

I see it every time I read of neighbors coming to the defense of neighbors, of communities banding together to hunt for a missing child or to comfort the parents of that child. I see it in the little kid down the street who bucked a lot of peer pressure to argue that he and his friends should not be making fun of the disabled kid next door. The world is filled with living saints who courageously choose to live according to principles of tolerance and love rather than of fear and hatred.

We can look at Mother Teresa as an example of holiness, but remember it was she who told us that we are all holy and that holiness is not confined to the few. We can look at Nelson Mandela and marvel at a man who would spend almost three decades of his life in prison for his beliefs, or at Martin Luther King, Jr., and the loneliness that he must have experienced in his quest for his people's rights. The world is filled with heroes if we want to see them. There are no "common men and women" in the eyes of God. There are only men and women. In my book about men, *The Grown-Up Man,* I listed many of the men who have affected my life positively. I encourage you to make a similar list for yourself.

HOW DO I BECOME A BETTER CHRISTIAN?

Here is the ultimate question: How do I become a better Christian? I don't presume to have all the answers, but I do have some suggestions based on my own personal work, as well as the work of many of our clients. I am convinced these are important. You can choose what might be challenging to you.

Dare To Think And Wonder

I have stressed this throughout this book, and I will do it again here. A lot of the evil in the world comes from ignorance, and a lot of ignorance comes from fear of the unknown. Dare to look at the contradictions in your thinking. We all have them. You aren't the only one. Ask yourself how you can embrace and have faith in the part of science that saves your daughter's or son's life, but then reject the part of science that seems to — but doesn't — contradict your religious beliefs. Ask yourself if you really believe that God wants us to remain in the dark. Ask yourself if killing the mind and heart and spirit of a child with fear of the new and with intellectual rigidity is what Jesus Christ wanted you to do.

Dare to create a home and family that is open to inquiry. Extremists will interpret this last statement to mean "a Godless, scientific, humanistic, un-Christian home," but that is not what I mean. In my heart, I believe that even the extremists out there know otherwise. I think they're just frightened, and perhaps too ashamed to admit it.

Create a home where children see parents learning, questioning, thinking and wondering so they will do the same. Create a home where religion is something that enhances life, where it supports people's spirits and ability to wonder instead of stifling them. Know that adults who have true faith do not have to emotionally and physically abuse their children in the name of their religion. They don't have to shame, control, restrict and constrict their children to get them to grow up to be kind, decent, caring human beings. They do most of it by example, with healthy limits and boundaries added all along the way.

Try to understand that solid faith, based on real love, is not afraid of questions. It is not afraid of differing opinions. If I am clear and comfortable in my beliefs, it isn't going to threaten me to know that some people believe otherwise. It won't threaten my role as a parent to have my children exposed to others' beliefs. I can trust that goodness will prevail if I live it in addition to preaching it.

Dare To Include All People

Racism is evil. Sexism is evil. Jesus Christ was absolutely clear in His acceptance of all people. He didn't give us any room to wiggle out of this one, to equivocate, intellectualize or deny. We humans have a very tough time with this. It goes back to our primitive ancestors who first met up in that valley thousands of years ago. We're afraid of each other, but that's our challenge. *Intolerance is evil.*

A couple of years ago the city of Dubuque, Iowa, decided that it was "too white" and it needed more racial diversity. The city fathers had a novel idea. Why not invite some black families to move to Dubuque? They did and some black families accepted their kind offer. In the spring of 1992 the Ku Klux Klan held a big rally in Dubuque, sort of a little welcoming committee for the black families. I think Jesus would have wept for those families. I believe He would have been outraged at the Klan. How dare we call ourselves civilized, I thought to myself. I am part of America and this happened in America, so I am partially responsible for it.

That was Dubuque, you argue. "It wouldn't happen in *my* town," you cry. Look around. It *is* happening in your town. It happens in all of our towns in one way or another. The world is getting way too small for us to be agentic all the time. We need to develop our communal side more than ever before. Fortunately, that is what Christianity is all about. Christianity is inclusive. Racists and "fear-mongers" promote exclusion. Look at how politicians try to exclude certain groups by playing on people's unconscious fears. If we as a people weren't so naive, we'd be furious with those politicians. Instead, we nod like sheep, our heads bobbing up and down, saying, "Yes, I love all people, but I don't want them in my neighborhood. After all, what will it do to my property value?"

Property value? These days we seem to be much more concerned about property values in America than we are about human values. I believe some of the most value-less folks around may be our most public figures — leaders running all over the country spouting off about values, when what they're really preaching is division, hatred and exclusion.

"Let's get the general public all riled up about some subgroup of society," they say. "Let's get them worked into a good, uncontrollable lather. Then let's promise to do something about that awful subgroup. Then let's get elected! Then we don't have to say any more publicly until the next election. That way we won't alienate the caring people too much. Then we can play on people's fears again, and we'll get elected again!" It's as easy as one, two, three, four.

If you are a Christian, this strategy won't work on you. If you are a Christian, you will be disgusted by politicians' attempts to play on our fears. You will be repulsed by the implication that some people are better than others. This is so contrary to the teachings of Jesus Christ that you will have no problem seeing the evil behind this sort of political message. But if you were never taught or allowed to think as a separate person, and if the people who raised you did not live by the values that they mouthed, then you will have a hard time separating evil political messages from healthy ones — a very hard time.

If you are truly a Christian, you no longer have certain choices. The most important one you no longer have is that of whom you should and shouldn't love. It's clear. We were commanded to love everyone, including our enemies. *Christ's message didn't exclude. His message included.* I believe this was His greatest challenge to us. It is the most difficult for us to try to carry out. Each of us struggles with this every day. We must continue to. This struggle is very good.

As you struggle, you will automatically be teaching your children to struggle with and embrace the same kind of love that Jesus taught. Think about it. Tolerance, inclusion, love and acceptance go hand-in-hand with knowledge. They are the opposite of fear. The more you broaden your own horizons by learning about the people in the next valley or across the ocean, the less fear you will have. Sure, you'll still have to struggle. The people in the next valley may not be two-headed monsters, but they may want the resources in a third valley just as much as you do. You may have to struggle with them, but you don't have to hate them, dehumanize them and then try to exterminate them in the name of God just because they want the same things that you want. All humans want the same things.

Dare to be tolerant. Dare to include people beyond your own tiny little corner of the world. Dare to teach your children, by your example, what Jesus Christ taught you — that Japanese, Chinese, Hispanic-Americans, African-Americans, Caucasians, Jews, the rich, the poor, the brilliant, the retarded, the fat, the thin, the powerful, the weak, and all the rest of humanity — are all equal in the eyes of the Lord. Dare to include.

Dare To Be Outraged

Outrage is about justice and social responsibility. Let me explain. By "dare to be outraged" I do not mean that we become filled with frightful rage and start hurting others around us "in the name of morality." I do not mean firebombing government buildings because of our anger. I do not mean ruthlessly shaming a fellow human being. I do not mean beating up someone because of who they are or what they represent. I do not mean killing someone. To be *outraged* is a very different notion than to be dangerously *enraged*. The latter is out of control, frightening, damaging. The former is grounded in moral principles, is powerful in a spiritual sense but not necessarily in an earthly sense, is constructive rather than destructive and comes out of a sense of internal wholeness.

Rage is destructive and it is fed by fear. During the Vietnam War, people became enraged and bombed buildings. Students were shot and killed. People hated. When a father or mother rages at a child because the child expresses prejudice toward another person, the parent only increases the child's fear and damages his spirit, which will cause the child to hate and fear even more. People who operate in extremes rage intensely and often. Whether they know it or not, there is no difference between "extreme left" and "extreme right" ragers. People who bomb health clinics that perform abortions are no different than people who bomb research centers that support an unjust war. They both have a moral principle for which they are struggling, and they are both using means that only hurt and damage. There are better and holier ways to get our messages across to each other.

Healthy outrage is constructive and it is fed by higher moral principles, not fear. Look at the outrage displayed by Candy

Lightner, the founder of Mothers Against Drunk Driving (MADD). She experienced one of the worst traumas that a human being can experience — the senseless, meaningless death of her own flesh and blood. Because of foolish laws that protected criminal drunk drivers, her daughter was killed. She was devastated, lost and horribly saddened by her loss. Then she became outraged. She channeled that outrage into one of the most courageous and effective campaigns ever conducted by a "common citizen." As a woman going up against the "good-old-boy" network of state legislatures at the time, she had a formidable, almost hopeless task, but her outrage kept her going.

Look at the outrage of Jesus Christ, who took on the entire religious establishment of His time. He gave to Caesar what was Caesar's. He never broke any civil laws. He was finally prosecuted on trumped-up charges and executed, but He never wavered in His spiritual convictions.

Look at the outrage of Martin Luther King, Jr., who was hated by whites as well as by extremist African-American groups.

Look at the outrage of an adult who discovers that he or she was sexually abused by a parent during childhood, works it through in therapy, and finally brings the truth to the family — only to be ostracized and told that he or she is crazy. The outrage as well as support from other healthy adults is what keeps that person going.

Outrage leads us to constructive action. Constructive action is powerful yet respectful. This kind of quiet power will scare unhealthy people, but that does not mean it is disrespectful. It just means it is scary to some. So if you are outraged at your child's intolerance, use that outrage constructively. Sit down with your child and let him or her know that you believe something else. Challenge your child to think about what he or she is saying. Let him have his intolerance, but let him know that you simply disagree. If you have a good parent-relationship with your child, he will eventually want to be like you. He will begin to wonder why the two of you agree on so many things, but disagree on this matter of intolerance. Because intolerance comes from ignorance and fear, your willingness to stay in relationship with your child but not to compromise your own values will let your child know that he does not have to fear losing your love. It will eventually create enough conflict inside of your child to help him see where his own intolerance is coming from. Then he will be able to release it.

Let your outrage about social injustice cause you to act. Contribute more money to worthy social causes. Write letters to your legislators. True, political action committees have an awful lot of power these days and many of us feel powerless to change government or society, but do it anyway. Sometimes it still works. Give some of your time and energy to people who need it and can't afford it. Yes, there are so many problems and you are only one person, but do it anyway. It might just make a difference somewhere. Above all, let your *outrage* work for you and for the good of others. Deal with your *rage* in therapy.

Take The Risk To Be Accountable And Forgive

To be accountable is to admit our humanity. To be accountable is to be spiritual. We can never improve ourselves and become more like God if we are unwilling to own our mistakes. It's a big risk. If I admit that I shouldn't have gone into your valley to steal your food, I will open myself up to shame, ridicule and even death. If I admit that I hurt you when you were a child, we will all be free to have our feelings about it. You may be angry at me for a long time. That won't be comfortable for me, but if we are ever to have a decent relationship, I must admit what I did without trying to weasel out of it. You can eventually break free from the painful memories even if I'm not accountable, but it will take a good deal longer.

Dare to forgive. Don't enable and thus allow an abuser to continue abusing you. That's easy. It doesn't require much internal struggle. To forgive as part of a process of making your own life and your children's lives safer — that takes effort.

Dare To Let Others Know You/Dare To Know Others

If isolation and alienation are evil, then it stands to reason that it is holy to take the risk to get to know other human beings. But it is scary to do so. We each wear a public mask. If that is all anyone sees of us, then we are isolated no matter how many friends we claim to have. It feels safer to hide behind our walls, but it also creates a lot of fear and hatred. Some people use their religion to hide from others. Some use their work to hide, some use chemicals or sex and others use their children.

Take the risk. Find people in your neighborhood, school or work with whom you can really share yourself. Take the risk to let your spouse or partner know what's really in your heart, even if it isn't pleasant or "nice." Part of true intimacy is to share this not-so-nice stuff, too. Linda and I work with countless couples who have been able to reclaim their relationships when they have risked getting to know each other, "warts and all." The pivotal moment in a couple's saving their marriage often comes when they admit that they hate each other and have been thinking about getting a divorce. Until they admit this, the secret that they both carry will kill the possibility of any true healing.

All human beings are drawn to each other but at times want to get away from each other. Running away or clinging and smothering are the extremes that block intimacy. Hanging in there and dealing with true feelings is what makes a deep relationship so enriching. Getting away when you need to and embracing when you choose to is the good part.

Take the risk to get to know your children as they are, not as you command them to be. You do not own them. They are not possessions. They are separate, individual human beings. They have their own hopes and fears and feelings and talents. Listen to them. Listen to their words and their feelings and their actions. You will discover there is an incredibly rewarding relationship just waiting.

Dare To Enjoy Your Senses And Your Body/Dare To Feel

Part of spirituality is celebration. I do not believe that life is meant to be continually morose and painful. There is certainly pain in life, but there is also joy. What if you grew up in a family that didn't value enjoyment? What will you do then? You may spend years feeling empty inside. You may feel ashamed of your desire to enjoy sunsets, smells, tastes and your own sexuality. You may be missing the sounds of your own children's laughter around your house.

It will be a risk for you to try to enjoy yourself. You will feel a lot of unhealthy guilt and shame. You may even have family members who imply that there is something wrong with you for wanting to enjoy your senses, but there isn't anything wrong. There is something very right. Remember the extremes? That is what becomes wrong — when you spend all your time trying to enjoy your senses to the detriment of the rest of your life. Smelling roses is not evil.

Remember, too, that as you learn to use your senses, you will be much less likely to make errors in judgment about people and things because you will be much more attuned to what is going on around you. The data you take in will be more accurate and complete. If you have never had a massage, go try one. If you don't like it, you don't have to go back. Have your partner give you a backrub and be as passive as you can be, just noticing how it feels to have someone touch you in a safe, non-sexual way.

Make your surroundings pleasant. If the naysayers in your house complain that flowers and pictures and decorations are a waste of money, tell them they are wrong. Tell them that our surroundings affect us very much and express us very much. People are happier, work more efficiently, are less stressed and get along with each other better when their surroundings are decorated nicely. It doesn't necessarily take a lot of money to make your home look beautiful and peaceful — it takes the risk to express yourself. If you walk into a home that is bare of decoration, you may often be right in assuming that the person who lives there is impoverished inside, lacking joy and life and spirit.

Dare to feel, too. Every feeling you experience has a purpose. Your anger protects you, your fear gives you wisdom, your shame lets you be accountable and spiritual, your pain tells you when something needs to be fixed or is about to be broken, your guilt gives you the energy to correct your mistakes, your sadness lets you heal from loss, your joy lets you celebrate your unique place in the universe and your loneliness lets you be with yourself so you can figure out who you are as well as giving you the drive to connect with others.

If the people around you are afraid of feeling, or if they shame you for having your feelings, then begin by looking for people who will support your feelings. You don't have to abandon your current family to start getting healthy. There are plenty of people around who want to feel their feelings and who will want to be around you as you learn to feel your emotions.

Dare To Heal And Grow Up

There are now several books on the market dealing with religious addiction. Father Leo Booth's *When God Becomes A Drug* is an excellent one. You might be especially enlightened by the 20 "toxic beliefs" outlined in the 1991 release, *Toxic Faith.* There are also many good books on painful families, abuse, incest and addictions, including Linda's and my *Adult Children: The Secrets Of Dysfunctional Families* and *An Adult Child's Guide To What's "Normal."* Despite the current backlash of negative sentiment against the recovery movement, as it has been called, there still is much good that can come from learning about these things. Because the fad has peaked does not mean that people are no longer being damaged in American families. Growing up in today's society is a very hard thing to do. I challenge you to do it anyway.

Healing from the ravages of an abusive childhood does not happen by prayer alone; I don't believe that this was Jesus' intent. Healing these wounds is scary and requires courage. It means talking to other people about it, which will induce shame. The only way to get rid of shame is to share it with others. It's the only way. If I were to choose what I believe to be the worst trait of a religiously-addicted family system, I would have to pick isolation. To break one's isolation is risky, but the damage that's done if it isn't broken is much worse.

Isolation in a family results in all kinds of emotional and physical pain. Isolated parents rely on their children to fill their emotional needs, which is called covert or emotional incest because it is so hurtful to children.

Dad may still be a child inside, having never grown up because of the abuse that he experienced in his family. He needs to grow up emotionally, but doesn't know how or isn't willing to take the risk. This Dad who can't meet his own social needs may rely on his child to fill those needs, which to some people looks really neat from the outside. They say how great it is that a Dad and his child are so close.

It isn't great. It is a betrayal of the child and it fills him with shame and rage that are buried deep inside. It teaches the child that adults are out to use kids, that adults can't be trusted, that adults are afraid to grow up and take social risks. It becomes self-perpetuating. The child grows up hopelessly enmeshed with the parent, feeling sorry for the parent, protecting the parent and feeling guilty when the child tries to break away from the parent to have his or her own adult life.

That is just one effect of isolation in religiously addicted families. There are many more. Growing up requires that we get our dependency needs met in healthy ways. It requires that we fill in some of the major shortages that we suffered as children, but we do it as adults. This means we can't put diapers on and be babies again, despite what some therapists claim. Growing up requires that we become accountable for our errors and that we think in adult ways.

Should I lash out and hate you, as if I were an enraged infant, just because you don't agree with my opinions? Or should I admit that it is my embarrassment and hurt that are causing my rage? Do I really believe that everyone is either good or evil? Is life really that simple? Should I punish you because you don't want to make love with me right now, should I try to force myself on you because I am "the head of the household" or should I grow up and stop being an abusive, self-centered baby? What do you think?

People sometimes believe that to grow up means to lose a certain "holy innocence" that can never be regained, so they resist growing up. I disagree. It is not holy innocence that we lose when we grow up. It is naivete. Healthy adults have hung onto their childlike openness and simplicity, but through the process of growing up they have become wiser, deeper and capable of much more love and intimacy. People who tell you to keep your childish naivete so that you can remain holy are selling you a bill of goods. If you look closely, they probably want a chunk of your money. Or maybe they want you to keep your mouth shut so they can do whatever they want to do to you or others without being accountable. Manipulative leaders really like that. Growing up doesn't hurt us or our children. Not growing up is what hurts.

Dare To Examine The Basis Of Your Beliefs

Are your beliefs based only on what you were told when you were four years old? Did you ever go through a searching period during which you questioned the beliefs that were told to you when you were little? Do you believe what you believe because of fear? Beliefs based on fear of punishment rather than on empathy and compassion for one's fellow human beings are usually childhood-based, immature beliefs. Most people would agree that a person is more evolved spiritually if he chooses not to kill because he believes that all people have a right to life, rather than choosing not to kill because he might go to hell for doing it.

In other words, we need to ask ourselves if our beliefs are grounded in our own personal struggles or if they are simply rote memorizations that we acquired when we were young children trying to please or appease the authority figures in our lives. We also need to ask ourselves if we are advocates of "moral rectitude" because we care about the welfare of humanity, or if it is because we simply want to save our own skins. People who act morally because they fear punishment will not be as likely to stick to their moral principles under stress as will people who act morally because of truly internalized moral principles.

Dare To Learn How To Parent

The most important legacy we can leave to society is how we treat our children. Severely abused and damaged little Adolf Hitler is proof enough of that. I have been involved with parent education in one form or another for the past 20 years, and I intend to continue for the next 20.

I didn't know much about being a parent when I first became one at age 23, and I find that whether new parents are 23 or 43, they are hungry for information about how to be parents.

We have so many good parent education programs throughout the country these days. Community colleges and adult education centers teach parenting skills all the time. Dare to admit that you don't have all the answers. It isn't enough to make a vow that you will raise your children more wisely than you were raised. If you weren't raised wisely, you won't know what wise parenting looks like. Try as you may, you'll wind up re-enacting your childhood experiences with your own children until you learn how to do it differently. How could it be otherwise?

I might be very motivated to repair the transmission of my car, but if nobody ever taught me how to do it, or if I was taught the incorrect way to do it, I won't be able to repair it. I'll make a mess of it despite my good intentions.

I have never met a parent who didn't have good *intentions,* but intentions aren't enough. We need *competence.* Competence only happens when we first admit that we don't know how to do something, we seek someone who knows how to do it, we submit to their teaching and expertise so that we can learn, then we learn and practice. In this age of instant communication and empty little "sound bites," people get the distorted idea that, if we can't learn it in 20 minutes, it isn't worth trying to learn. What a setup for fear and ignorance.

Dare to admit you aren't perfect and that you don't know it all. Dare to become a better parent. Dare to ask other parents how they handle child-rearing problems. You don't have to do it the way they do, but for goodness sake, how will you ever learn new ways of parenting if you never ask and discuss? You won't. There is nothing shameful about not knowing how to handle children. All of us have problems and questions about our kids. Parents who are willing to admit their shortcomings and then do something about them become great parents. Parents who fear admitting their shortcomings become awful parents. The children of awful parents grow up to be angry, empty, lonely and frightened inside. It is hard to be a good Christian when you always feel that way.

Dare To Care

To be a good person — Muslim, Buddhist, Jew, atheist, Christian — *means to care.* It isn't easy to care. It's much easier in certain ways not to care. When we care, we can't hate quite as much. When we care, we can't fear quite as much. When we care, we give up certain things that we could have if we didn't care. Sometimes when we care, we risk being ostracized by our friends and relatives. We can even risk death, but to be a Christian means to care, regardless of the consequences.

When we dare to care we make a commitment to live a more challenging life than if we don't dare to care. We make a commitment to become more tolerant of differences. We make a commitment to share our energy or resources with people less fortunate than ourselves. We make a commitment to love as much as we can without being abused continually in the process. We make a commitment to keep growing.

It is tempting to every human being to hoard what we have acquired and achieved once we have it, especially if we started out in life with very little. Hoarding ultimately backfires. Spiritual people know that the gifts they have achieved in life are in part just that — they are gifts. Spiritual people are grateful for what they have as well as for what they don't have, and they therefore find it easier not to hoard. Regardless of how hard you have worked for what you have achieved, at least a small part of what you have achieved is a gift that was given to you by your parents, your Creator, Fate, or the Universe. Arrogant people believe every last bit of what they have is their own doing. People who are stuck in their victim role believe they have no say at all in what happens to them. Somewhere in between these two extremes is the truth.

Share some of what you have with someone else. I don't believe you have to give it all away and go about in sackcloth and ashes, but share some of it. Ask your friend who is wearing pain on his face today if he is in pain. He may not want to discuss it, so just go on and allow him his privacy and dignity. Maybe he does want to discuss it and didn't know how to reach out. You don't have to become his therapist just because you care. You don't have to let him manipulate you into listening over and over to the same sad tale so that he never has to grow up, but surely we can take the time now and then to care.

It is a struggle and a challenge to care for one another. It can be a hassle in our busy, overworked society, but our society won't be around forever if we lose the ability to care. If we lose that, we'll simply revert back to the days when we roamed the planet in nomadic bands of hungry people who tried for thousands of years to wipe out the other hungry people so we could take it all. We all know where that almost led us — to total and absolute nuclear destruction.

CHAPTER 14

To Think And Hope

For everyone who asks receives, and he who seeks finds, and to him who knocks it will be opened.
Matthew 7:8

Think And Come Out Of The Darkness

By including Doubting Thomas in his group, Jesus Christ was telling us that it is okay to use our powers of reason, analysis and critical thinking. He was telling us it is part of the dignity and worth of being human that we strive to know, wonder, question and have awe about the universe.

Where would we be now if we hadn't been thinking and wondering and questioning across the centuries? Think of all the humane, caring, life-enhancing things we would still be without. Think of all the tortured bodies and minds that have been helped by medical advances. Think of all the terrible diseases that can now be treated because someone dared to think and wonder. Think of all the children whose parents no longer abuse them because someone dared to change the system. As Catholic philosopher Michael Novak wrote in *Belief And Unbelief,* human beings have an innate desire to know. It is this exercise of our God-given intellectual powers that makes us unique.

Think of all the accumulated wisdom in our culture — knowledge we simply take for granted — that was gained at such a terrible cost to those who dared to think it and search for it. What I'm wondering is this: Who are we persecuting, shaming and killing today, either literally or emotionally, because of what they believe? How will people 2,000 years from now look back at us? Will they sit in classrooms of the future and snicker at our intellectual narrowness, appalled at our brutish ignorance and insensitivity to the pioneers of our time who believed things that were just too scary for us to believe?

Whose spirits and souls are we killing daily as we lash out at our teenagers and young adults when they simply ask questions about what they were told when they were four years old? Isn't it part of the holiness of becoming a more spiritually deep person to ask questions?

I don't believe Christ wanted us to remain in pain, ignorance and darkness. I don't believe He wanted us to remain barbaric. I have the strong hunch that what Christ wanted us to do is to love one another. I also believe He wanted us to learn all we can about the workings of the universe around us. With each new bit of information we learn, we understand ourselves more, we understand creation more and we are therefore able to have a closer relationship with God.

We learned in history classes that one way tyrants kept people under control over the centuries was to keep them in the darkness of ignorance. In other words, if we let people ask one question, then they ask another one. Then another and another. Pretty soon we have a populace that's thinking. Once the people start to think, we risk losing control over them. Eventually they'll hold us accountable, which is the last thing that a tyrant wants. Thinking and asking questions are part of being spiritual, moral and holy.

For those of you who are learning to wonder, I would like to list a few of the many questions that I, my clients and thousands of others have asked themselves at one time or another. As you read through them, I ask you one thing. Please notice how you *feel* as you read them, what you *think* as you read them and anything they might prompt you to *do* after reading them. Please remember that Jesus Christ asked us to think. He spoke in parables that made people think. He challenged the conventional wisdom of His day. Many people feared or hated Him because of the questions He asked. He used His brain, and by doing so I believe He was asking us to also use ours.

- Did Christ mean we should feel better than everyone else because we have a degree in medicine, law or psychology?
- Did He say that we are better than everyone else because we make less money than our neighbor?
- Did He say that we have no dignity because we are a thief, a prostitute or a bum?
- Why did Christ hang around thieves, prostitutes and bums? Why didn't He just hang around "holy" men?
- Did He say that it wasn't okay to have a human body? Was it when He said "This is my body. This is my blood?"
- If Christ was perfect, and if He was God, why didn't He just wave a magic wand and make his persecutors disappear?
- If He was God and God's Son, why did He despair and feel so terribly alone and forsaken just before His crucifixion?

- Did Christ say that it was good to take people's money in His name and then spend it on mansions and limousines?
- Did He tell us to preach His teachings publicly while privately doing the opposite?
- Did He say that the way to get to heaven was to do good works in the community so that we look good in public, but ignore the emotional needs of our spouse and children at home?
- Does everyone who does not belong to my religion really go to hell for all eternity? Could a loving, forgiving God really do that?
- If I practice my religious rituals faithfully, but don't live my faith, am I a holy person? Can I get to heaven if I practice the rituals but cheat and lie and hate others the rest of the time?
- Which is more important in the eyes of God: to go to church every week or to respect myself and others, respect and love the planet on which I live and respect and love the people in my life?
- Can a truly good person hate? Am I bad if I hate my brother or sister or father or mother now and then when they do something that makes me really angry?
- Am I bad if I like sex?
- Am I good if I don't like sex?
- Is a child who asks questions and wonders about religion, the universe and my values a bad child? An immoral child? A disrespectful child?
- What if some of the demons that Christ cast out weren't really demons? What if some of those people were simply psychotic, mentally ill due to an imbalance of brain chemicals? What if Christ's miracle was that He cured the imbalance of brain chemicals in that person's brain? Would it be any less of a miracle? Would it shake the foundations of my faith to the very core if this were true?

- Will today's scientists go to hell for proposing the Big Bang Theory?
- Am I abusing my children because I prevent them from thinking and wondering and questioning? If so, am I doing it because I am afraid?

Let's Hope

I don't know what will happen to the people on this planet 50 years from now or 2,000 years from now. As I wrote earlier, I have enough trouble just keeping up with my own household and neighborhood here in Minnesota. I don't know if the ozone layer will disappear and we will all be fried like crepes on a skillet, if our air and water will eventually poison us all, or if an airborne AIDS-type virus will evolve and quickly exterminate all of us without a moment's notice. I hope these things won't happen. In fact I hope other more positive things do happen. I hope we find a cure for AIDS, whether it be HIV-related or a new strain. I hope our religious institutions become more accountable for the abuses that they perpetuate. I hope we Americans become less greedy, self-centered and violent as a nation. I hope the gap between rich and poor in the world grows smaller.

While I consider myself an optimist at heart, I am also a realist. I know that people have been fighting over property rights in the Middle East for centuries, which means that it may go on for a few more centuries. I know that the hatred between Catholics and Protestants in Northern Ireland has gone on for so long that it has become an ingrained way of life. I know that we have had problems of poverty and violence and sexism and racism in America for so long that at times change seems hopeless. I know these things.

I reluctantly let go of my Pollyannish beliefs about the world somewhere in my mid-30s, and I feel like a much better person for having done so. Growing up and becoming realistic isn't the same thing as becoming bitter and cynical. I believe that human history is evolving in a positive direction despite all of our sociocultural errors.

The Roman Catholic Church gave us Torquemada and the Spanish Inquisition, but it also gave us one of the most beloved men in world history — Pope John XXIII. I have faith in God and in humanity. Horrendous spiritual abuses gave rise to Martin Luther and the Reformation. Years of slavery and human suffering gave rise to the civil rights movement. Women finally got the right to vote. Men are beginning to be accountable for their offender behavior. The victims of Father James Porter's sexual crimes have bonded together in love and support for all to see, which has already made my job as a psychologist much easier. When someone takes a risk to share their shame and pain, someone else feels just a little bit more free to deal with theirs. These are all acts of Christian love.

I was heartened and relieved to read of the 70 leaders from Minneapolis-St. Paul churches who got together after the Los Angeles riots "to take concrete steps to deal with the pernicious reality of racism." They represented, among others, Protestants, Roman Catholics and Jews. Carolyn Hendrixson of the Minneapolis Council Of Churches said, "If you read the Bible, we should be the group that deals with racism." She added later, "They want to blame the problems on the government or poverty. Those are issues, but the root cause is racism."

If you have come far enough in this book to be reading this last chapter, then you must have asked yourself a question or two. Even if some of what I have written here makes you angry or afraid, at least you took the risk to think about it. I don't ask or expect that anyone agree with everything I have written here. I don't ask or expect anything from the reader, but I can hope. I hope that by reading this book some of you will have a stronger faith in what Jesus Christ was trying to teach us. I hope that you were challenged to think or feel or do something differently. I hope that something in this book will make your life better and that it will make the lives of others better.

As human beings and as Christians we have free will and we have choices. That is what I believe. We can choose to be ignorant and afraid. We can choose to reject the truth that is right in front of our noses. We can choose to be violent and discriminatory. We can choose to let our fear turn into hatred and abuse. Or we can pull together and become enlightened — we can come into the Light. Ernest Becker was right. We are not vicious animals. It is part of being human to fear other humans, but is part of being holy to go beyond the fear. I pray that we let the Spirit into our souls.

APPENDIX

MY OWN RELIGIOUS HISTORY

Because religion is such a personal thing for each of us, I feel it is only fair for the reader to know a little bit about me and my personal history. I am not a theologian, nor am I a minister or priest. I am a psychologist by profession, but I am also just another human being trying to make sense out of my life. I try to love my wife, children, friends and associates as best I can, and I am challenged by questions of belief and religion as much as the next person. I belong to a Christian church.

I grew up in the San Francisco Bay area. I have an older sister and an older brother. My father was an attorney who, interestingly, never went to college. He went to law school at night during the Depression while working during the day, and he went on to have quite a distinguished career later in his life. My mother was a typical 1950s suburban housewife who was active in Cub Scouts and Girl Scouts, in raising us and in being a wife to my father. All three of the Friel children were successful students in school. We all graduated from college and have attended graduate school of one sort or another in our adult lives. On the surface, at least to some of the folks we encountered as we were growing up, ours was a normal, healthy, typical California family. (Some might argue that this last statement is an oxymoron, but we'll leave that for another book.)

Both of my parents were raised as Mormons in Utah, and both of them moved to the San Francisco Bay area in the early 1930s to pursue their careers and/or make their fortunes. They met at a Mormon Church function, dated, fell in love and got married. They apparently did not have a strong commitment to the Mormon faith. When they moved across the Golden Gate Bridge to Marin County for the purpose of raising their children in a more idyllic environment, there was no Mormon Church to be had so we simply attended an Episcopal Church from before I was born until many years later.

My first memories of church, doctrine, dogma and the like were from a small Low-Episcopal Church in a quaint little town with bucolic, tree-lined streets that was 35 minutes from downtown San Francisco. My earliest memories of church, religion and Christianity were warm and safe and comfortable. I remember everyone from our little town picking spring flowers from our gardens and carrying them with excitement and anticipation to the church on Easter Sunday morning to make a huge cross of flowers to commemorate Christ's Resurrection. We brought daffodils and sweet-smelling lilacs, as I recall. In fact, I still get tearful when I hear the traditional Protestant hymns that we sang at that church. It felt like a good place to worship. I attended the typical Sunday school program of that day and learned about the life of Christ just as all Sunday school kids do. The people who taught those classes were respectful of children and seemed to understand how children's minds worked. I learned and believed without feeling frightened or intimidated. It was a very positive experience for me, as I look back on it.

My childhood progressed seemingly quite normally. When my older sister was ready to enter high school, my parents made the decision to send us to the local Catholic high school because it had a much better reputation for quality education than did the public high schools. By the time my sister and brother were both in high school they had learned enough about Catholicism to decide to become Catholics. They did so after the typical training and education required at the time. Their excitement and enthusiasm for the church was intoxicating, and at the age of 14, when I was in the eighth grade, I, too, became a Catholic. Within a couple of years, my parents also joined the Catholic Church.

To some, this evolution from Mormon to Episcopal to Catholic may seem like an odd one. When my parents were children, it was well-known to them that Mormons disliked Catholics and vice versa, yet here they were, a couple who went all the way back to Salt Lake City to get married in the Mormon Temple, who were baptized in the Catholic Church and who did so after a great deal of effort, money and agony. My father had been married briefly prior to his marriage to my mother and it took months of private investigation to track down his ex-spouse and document the details of that first marriage. It was a very emotional and joyous time indeed the day that they were allowed into the Church.

As for me, the Catholic Church became a compulsive and guilt-ridden experience that simply reinforced the underlying deep pain that I was already feeling by the time I reached high school. Beneath the normality and apparent health of my family, there lay a hidden disease that did extensive damage to all of us.

My father had become an alcoholic early in his adulthood — a response to his genetic predisposition to the disease, and also a response to the severe emotional abuse he experienced when he was growing up in Utah. By the time I was in the first or second grade, my mother also became chemically dependent — first on drugs that her psychiatrist gave her to treat the pain of living with an alcoholic and eventually on alcohol itself. I found out much later that her father had also been alcoholic.

As a child of two alcoholic parents I was already displaying most of the now well-known characteristics of such children. In high school, I looked good on the outside but was hurting terribly on the inside. I was a model child during the day and then got into all kinds of minor trouble at night and on weekends. I had difficulty concentrating. I was angry and impulsive. I was socially incompetent. I turned to chemicals in high school to medicate that pain and to try to fit in. High school was a horrible experience for me. The Catholicism that was so joyously embraced by my parents and siblings became more and more of a trap for me. Attending church became an extension of being a "good little boy" and a "dutiful rule-follower." It became an obsessive, ritualized experience that was numbing and spiritually murderous for me.

One of the few positive religious experiences I had in high school came from Father Francis Lacey's religion classes at Marin Catholic High School. High school kids aren't very interested in religion, but somehow he let Jesus' life come alive for me despite my "teenager-hood" and my pain. I remember him coming to my house in the midst of one of my parents' alcoholic crises, trying to help and being almost as lost as the rest of us. But I remember that he tried. Back then I was angry at him, ashamed that he was witnessing my sick family. I was angry at Christianity, at my family and at myself, and I didn't even know it. Now I feel grateful that he tried to get me to think and that he tried to help my alcoholic family.

My brother and I both went on to attend the University of San Francisco, a Jesuit institution that was understandably quite liberal in its theological teachings. I was a dutiful but alcoholic student who was trying desperately to fit in somewhere, but it just wasn't happening. On the outside I was gregarious and fun-loving, but on the inside I was lonely, isolated and afraid. I certainly did not take theology or philosophy seriously for the most part, yet there was one course and one Jesuit priest who touched my mind indelibly. I am sad that I can't remember his name to give him credit for the impact that he had on me, but those things happen. What I do remember is that it was a course with a title like "Christ The Man." His way of teaching it eventually allowed me to get past my hurt and pain and religious compulsivity so I could again feel safe and warm and comfortable with Christianity after many years of rejecting any and all religious dogma and belief.

My ex-wife and I were married in the Catholic Church when I was 20 years old, between my sophomore and junior years in college. Two years later we moved to the East Coast to go to graduate school, where we both drifted away from Catholicism. We had two beautiful daughters whom we love dearly. We moved to Minnesota. Our lives and our marriage started to crumble around us. We were eventually divorced. Approximately four years later my life took its greatest downturn. I lost my job, my health, my dignity and any sense of direction, purpose or meaning in life. Throughout all of that pain and misery I never once considered the possibility of a Higher Power in my life until, as so often happens, it got so bad that the concept of a Higher Power was the only thread left for me to hang onto.

Somewhere in my mid-30s I finally surrendered to all of the fear, pain and agony, and shame, guilt and emptiness that I had been carrying around since I was a little boy. In terror and with a huge sense of failure, I joined a therapy group and eventually a 12-Step recovery group for alcoholism. I had a Ph.D. in psychology, I was everybody else's helper and rescuer, I had a monumental amount of shame because I couldn't fix myself without others' help. I finally sat in a circle with other wounded people and felt the first healing twinges of spirituality that I had felt since those early days as a little boy who brought the daffodils and lilacs to the Episcopal Church on Easter Sunday morning. It was a wonder for me to behold.

Like so many recovering people, accepting the concept of a Higher Power was a grating, scraping, annoying, frightening and painfully slow process. I gradually realized that I had been emotionally abused as a child by my parents' alcoholism and the accompanying crisis and trauma that it produced. It dawned on me one day that it makes perfect sense for a child to not want to trust a Higher Power when his first "Higher Powers," his parents, hurt him so much. It also dawned on me that the "old" Catholic Church with its rigid rules and shame and guilt had been abusive. I finally realized that a religion which does not respect children produces children who fear and hate the concept of God that is taught to them. As I experienced the weekly healing of therapy and other support over the ensuing months, I also began to realize that what had happened to me in the past did not have to dictate what was to happen to me in the present.

By this time I was remarried to Linda, a woman who had also grown up in an abusive, alcoholic home. She is my wife, my partner, my best friend, my lover, my confidant, the co-author of our first two books on dysfunctional families. She is a person of remarkable insight, inner beauty, strength, power, sensitivity and wisdom. She is also a psychologist, but we can forgive her that error.

I realized that for the first time in my life, I liked who I was. I liked the life that Linda and I were making for ourselves, I liked being in recovery and I liked what I did for a living. I had always loved and liked my children, but I now began to see that there was more to being a parent than just feeling strongly about them. I began to like Linda's son from her first marriage. I began to have friendships that were clear and clean and healthy. I began to have true self-esteem rather than grandiosity based on fear and denial of my inner pain. And then I began to understand what the story of Christ and the New Testament was all about.

My spirituality began when I was a little boy attending that Episcopal Church. I hung onto what little of it I could by communing with nature in the redwood forests and the coastal beaches of northern California. I could sit on the top of a coastal mountain or at the edge of the Pacific Ocean. I could look up at the vastness and expanse of the universe on a clear, starry night. In that way I could hang onto a thin, fragile thread of spirituality that kept me going and kept me connected to some vague concept of a Higher Power.

What happened in my recovery was that I realized spirituality doesn't come from memorizing rules and regulations. It doesn't come from practicing empty rituals while emotionally bleeding inside. I realized that spirituality begins with the experience of human beings treating each other with dignity, respect, warmth, tolerance and openness. I realized that a circle of people exposing their strengths and weaknesses to each other produced a power and energy in the room that can only be described as holy.

One day I woke up and had a flashback to that class on "Christ The Man" that had somehow touched my unconscious mind. A flood of feelings, insights and memories swept into consciousness.

Then it hit me. Christ's life and his powerful message were very simple. It wasn't filled with rules and regulations, and hatred, fear and intolerance. Christ Himself wasn't an abstract, incomprehensible, arrogant, grandiose, fearful, threatening person. The whole point of Christ's life and message was so simple that it took all of those years of pain and dysfunction for me to finally see it.

The process of healing from the wounds of childhood abuse is extremely painful. I have the utmost respect and admiration for anyone who chooses to stop denying their pain and begin that healing process. For me, it was a minimum of seven years of active struggle and of painful, addictive, damaging relationships in which I did damage and in which others damaged me. It included therapy in which I had to face that dark pit of fear and emptiness that Linda and I now help our clients face. It included dredging up all of the abuse and feeling it again. It included expressing hurt, fear, loneliness and anger at the people who hurt me. For a time, I hated both of my parents for what they did to me and my siblings, but slowly things started to get better. Because children always blame and shame themselves when they are treated abusively, I needed to learn to separate what was done to me from who I was. I also started to separate who I was then from who I am now, which is equally important.

My father died in 1986 and my mother died in 1987. Neither of them ever got into recovery *per se*, although for medical reasons they did stop using chemicals. I believe my father was able to surrender a little bit as he neared death, although he was never able to really deal with his feelings or to be close to others emotionally. The damage that was done to him by his family was apparently just too great, and the professional help that is now available was not around when he could have benefited from it most. My mother spent the last year of her life alone with her nurse, to whom she became very attached. In that year she began to show some long sought-after peace and serenity. She was able to talk about life and death and to share bits and pieces of her pain in a somewhat guarded way. She, too, went to her death in a great deal of denial about her own addictions and the abuse and neglect that she experienced as a little girl.

I am thankful that they were both able to be together in their final years, and that they both got to die at home as they fought so strongly to do. I would have liked it if they had found recovery, but that is not always possible. I no longer hate them for what they did because I was able to share those feelings with other people who understood that we can hate someone and love them at the same time. I know that I would never have been able to be at my mother's bedside when she died had I not done that emotional healing work prior to her death. It would have been just too scary to get that close to her again.

I hope that whatever work I have done on myself over the years will make it just a little bit easier for my own children to work through their pain as they grow up and face it in their adulthoods.

As far as religion goes, my parents died as clear, strong, practicing Catholics. I believe their religion helped them a lot, especially in their final years. My sister and brother are still Catholics, and I belong to a Presbyterian Church. When we sing those Protestant hymns, especially on Easter, I have a huge flood of good memories that connect back to that little Episcopal Church in California.

Born in March of 1947, I am 46 years old right now, and in some ways I am just beginning my life. I have enough recovery to feel whole and to feel healthy in my marriage and in my relationships with my children, my friends and myself. I do not believe that I "have arrived," because I know the moment I believe that, I will have begun my slide back into the darkness and pain and denial of my past. I am beginning to be very grateful for who I am and for what I have in this life. I know that my life is fragile and that every day of feeling whole and healthy is a gift to me.

I am also beginning to feel what healthy humility is like, as opposed to groveling and self-deprecation or false pride and grandiosity. I am beginning to understand what Christ was trying to tell us by His example and by His life, as opposed to what we humans have done with His message over the centuries since His death. And I am beginning to understand why the tolerance of other people's beliefs, and of other people's paths to recovery and spirituality, must be respected regardless of what I personally believe.

NOTES

Except as noted, all Bible quotations are from **The New King James Version** (Nashville: Thomas Nelson Publishers, 1982).

Preface

1. Stone, O., **Wall Street** (20th Century Fox Film Corporation in association with American Entertainment Partners LP.).
2. This quote from Rodney King was on the cover of *Time* magazine, the May 11, 1992 issue.
3. Friel, J.C., **The Grown-Up Man: Heroes, Healing, Honor, Hurt, Hope** (Deerfield Beach, FL: Health Communications, Inc., 1991).
4. Hagberg, J.O. & Guelich, R.A., **The Critical Journey: Stages In The Life Of Faith** (Dallas: Word Publishing, 1989), 2.

1. My First Encounter With "Christian" Hatred

1. "Five Held In Alleged Gay-Bashing Incident," *Minneapolis Star Tribune*, July 28, 1992.

2. The Heights Of Spirit

1. Flowers, B.S. (Ed.), **Joseph Campbell: The Power Of Myth, With Bill Moyers** (New York: Doubleday, 1988), 258.

2. De Chardin, P.T., **The Evolution Of Chastity** (London: William Collins Sons & Co. Ltd., 1972).

3. Coles, R., **The Spiritual Life Of Children** (Boston: Houghton Mifflin Company, 1990), 335. Coles' book, as is true of all his writing, is a magnificent piece of work and gives the reader a meticulous and compassionate look at children's spiritual development across many cultures.

4. The information contained in this section is based on my four years of Ph.D. work and several years of teaching developmental psychology, especially the work of Piaget, Erik Erikson, Bruner and Chomsky. Interested readers may want to refer to any good college-level text in that field.

5. The following references offer a somewhat complex but good initiation to the works of Swiss psychologist Jean Piaget:

Piaget, J., **The Language And Thought Of The Child** (New York: Harcourt Brace, 1926).

Piaget, J., **The Child's Conception Of Numbers** (New York: Harcourt Brace, 1929).

Piaget, J., **The Psychology Of Intelligence** (New York: Harcourt Brace, 1950).

Flavell, J.H., **The Developmental Psychology Of Jean Piaget** (Princeton, NJ: Van Nostrand Company, Inc., 1963).

6. Rahner, K., **The Spirit In The Church** (New York: The Seabury Press, 1979), 12.

7. Ibid., 11.

8. Didier, C.W., "Spiritual Serendipity." Sermon given at House of Hope Presbyterian Church, St. Paul, MN, March 15, 1992.

9. May, G.G., **Addiction And Grace** (New York: Harper & Row, 1988), 126.

10. Borg, M.J., **Jesus: A New Vision** (San Francisco: Harper & Row, 1987), 191.

3. In The Beginning

1. Becker, E., **Escape From Evil** (New York: The Free Press, 1975), 169.
2. Bakan, D., **The Duality Of Human Existence** (Chicago: Rand McNally, 1966).
3. Adler, M., **Truth In Religion: The Plurality Of Religions And The Unity Of Truth** (New York: Macmillan Publishing Company, 1990), 38.
4. Smith, W.C., **The Meaning And End Of Religion** (New York: Macmillan Publishing Company, 1963).
5. See the *Newsweek* cover story from the July 16, 1990 issue.
6. deMause, L., **The History Of Childhood** (New York: Psychohistory Press, 1974).

4. Hell On Earth: How Our Spirits Get Damaged

1. Kaufman, G., **Shame: The Power Of Caring** (Cambridge: Schenkman Publishing Co., 1980).
2. "EVIL — Does It Exist, Or Do Bad Things Just Happen?" *Time*, June 10, 1991.
3. "The Rekindling Of HELL — Record Numbers Of Americans Now Believe In A Netherworld, And In A Wide Variety Of After-Death Punishments." *U.S. News & World Report*, March 25, 1991. In a Gallup Poll cited in the article, 78% of Americans said they believed in heaven and 60% in hell. Of course, 78% also believed they had a good chance of going to heaven while only 4% thought they might go to hell.
4. **Judgment,** Home Box Office Films.
5. Information on the "Father Porter Case" is from the following sources:

Woodward, K.L., Friday, C. & Springen, K., "The Sins Of The Father," *Newsweek*, June 1, 1992.

Mehren, E., "Unleashed Memories," *Los Angeles Times,* June 7, 1992.

PrimeTime Live, ABC, Diane Sawyer reporting, July 1992.

6. Berry, J., **Lead Us Not Into Temptation** (New York: Doubleday, 1992).

7. Allen, M.S., "Abuse By Clergy," *Minneapolis Star Tribune,* July 4, 1992.

8. Schoener, G., "Prevention And Intervention In Cases Of Professional Misconduct: Psychology Lags Behind," *Minnesota Psychologist,* May 1992, 9.

9. The quote by Gary Schoener is from the *Minneapolis Star Tribune,* August 1992. Information for this section was also taken from CNN's **Sonya Live,** with Sonya Friedman, on August 13, 1992. It was noted that the American Medical Association was invited to send a representative to the television studio for the program, but declined.

10. Osterreich, L. & Shirer, K., "Understanding Abuse: Spouse & Partner Abuse," "Understanding Abuse And Neglect" and "Understanding Abuse: Rape, An Act Of Aggression," Iowa State University, University Extension, April 1992.

11. Horton, A.L. & Williamson, J.A., **Abuse And Religion: When Praying Isn't Enough** (Lexington, MA: Lexington Books, 1988). This is an excellent resource for professionals. It is comprised of research and theory articles on religion, abuse and counseling issues.

12. Borg, M.J., **Jesus: A New Vision,** 133-135.

13. Statistics on hunger are from *U.S. News And World Report,* October 21, 1991, 18.

14. Morganthau, T., "The Price Of Neglect," *Newsweek,* May 11, 1992.

15. Quote from Mother Teresa was reported in the *Minneapolis Star Tribune,* August 1992.

5. If Jesus Christ Had Wanted Us To Think, He Would Have Spoken To Us In Parables

1. See Note Five from Chapter Two.

2. The best book I have seen, written by Einstein himself for the general public, is **Relativity: The Special And The General Theory, A Popular Exposition** (New York: Crown Publishers, 1961).

3. Adler, M., **Truth In Religion,** 87-88.

6. Daddy, What's A Myth?

1. **History Of The George Washington Bicentennial Celebration.** Published in three volumes by the United States George Washington Bicentennial Commission, 1932.

7. Beliefs, Re-Enactments And "The Vow"

1. For popular discussions of Neanderthal Man, see Fischman, J., "Hard Evidence," *Discover,* February 19, 1992, and "Early Man: A Radical View Of Where We Came From," *U.S. News & World Report,* September 16, 1991.

2. Sheler, J.L. & Schrof, J.M., "The Creation," *U.S. News & World Report,* December 23, 1991.

3. Smith, H., **The Religions Of Man** (New York: Harper & Row, 1986), 419-420.

4. Madden, M.C., **The Power To Bless: Healing And Wholeness Through Understanding** (Nashville, TN: Broadman Press, 1970), 18.

5. Ibid., 19.

6. Two of Alice Miller's best-known works are: **Thou Shalt Not Be Aware: Society's Betrayal Of The Child** (1984), and **For Your Own Good: Hidden Cruelty In Child-rearing And The Roots Of Violence,** (New York: Farrar Strauss Giroux, 1983).

7. For example, see Note 11 from Chapter Four.

8. Petrie, A. & Petrie, J., **Mother Teresa** (Petrie Productions, Inc., 1985).

9. The entire Prayer For Serenity by Reinhold Niebuhr is: God, grant me the serenity to accept the things I cannot change, courage to change the things I can, and the wisdom to know the difference — living one day at a time, enjoying one moment at a time — accepting hardship as a pathway to peace — taking, as Jesus did, this sinful world as it is, not as I would have it — trusting that You will make all things right if I surrender to Your will — so that I may be reasonably happy in this life and supremely happy with You forever in the next.

8. Are Our Bodies Evil?

1. See Note Six in Chapter Three
2. Nelson, J.B., **Embodiment** (Minneapolis: Augsburg Publishing House, 1978). This is one of the most thoughtful books on modern Christianity to date, covering a number of very difficult theological questions, including sexuality and spirituality.
3. deChardin, P.T., **The Divine Milieu** (New York: Harper & Row, 1960), 105.
4. Ibid., 108.
5. Ibid., 108.

9. Sex, Sexual Abuse And Christianity

1. Statistics from The American Humane Association were cited in Fuller, J., Matheny, D. & Ode, K., "Child Sexual Abuse," *Minneapolis Star Tribune,* February 2, 1991.
2. "Sex And Religion: Churches, The Bible And Furor Over Modern Sexuality," *U.S. News And World Report,* June 10, 1991.
3. Nelson, J.B., **Embodiment,** 47.
4. Kaminer, W., **I'm Dysfunctional, You're Dysfunctional: The Recovery Movement And Other Self-Help Fashions** (New York: Addison-Wesley Publishing Co., 1992). A humorous, scathing, thoughtful critique of everything from recovery to *est* and beyond. This kind of

critique is sorely needed, especially for those of us in recovery who tend to get overly invested in pet theories or gurus.

5. Satir, V., **Conjoint Family Therapy** (Palo Alto, CA: Science And Behavior Books, 1967).

6. Vanderbilt, H., "Incest: A Chilling Report," *Lear's*, February 1992.

7. Johnson, C., **Lucky In Love** (New York: Viking, 1992).

8. Koestenbaum, P., **Existential Sexuality: Choosing To Love** (Englewood Cliffs, NJ: Prentice-Hall, 1974).

9. I have searched for this reference but have been unable to find it. The biologist was a woman, I believe, and the article was in either *Omni* or *Discover* magazines, sometime in 1992.

10. MacMurray, J., **Reason And Emotion** (London: Faber & Faber, 1935), 39.

11. De Chardin, P.T., **Human Energy** (London: William Collins Sons & Co. Ltd., 1969). The illusion is that we can become totally absorbed in each other, thereby creating a self-sustaining two-person universe. This does not work from a psychological standpoint, nor does it from a theological one. Teilhard says that the only way out of this dilemma is for the couple to eventually orient themselves outside of the relationship, to the greater society at large and eventually to God.

10. The Pharisees And Hypocrites: Shame, Fear, Prejudice And Ignorance

1. Smith, H., **The Religions Of Man,** 421.

2. Ibid., 421

3. Statistics are from Handgun Control and the Bureau Of Justice Statistics, reported in *Newsweek*, April 8, 1991, 31.

4. Hilts, P.J., "Study Shows Gunfire Mowing Down Teens," *St. Paul Pioneer Press*, June 10, 1992.

5. *USA Today*, July 31-August 2, 1992.

6. Loetscher, L.A., **A Brief History Of The Presbyterians** (Philadelphia: Westminster Press, 1978).

11. Sin, Accountability And Forgiveness

1. Oates, W.E., **The Psychology Of Religion** (Waco, TX: Word Books, 1973), 211.

2. Becker, E., **The Denial Of Death** (New York: Free Press, 1973), 196.

3. Petrie, A. & Petrie, J., **Mother Teresa.**

4. For example, Minuchin, S., **Families And Family Therapy** (Cambridge: Harvard University Press, 1974), or Bowen, M., **Family Therapy In Clinical Practice** (New York: Jason Aronsen, 1978).

12. Embracing The Many Faces Of Prayer

1. "Talking To God: An Intimate Look At The Way We Pray," *Newsweek*, January 6, 1992.

2. Schleiermacher, F., **On Religion: Speeches To Its Cultured Despisers** (Cambridge University Press, 1988).

3. Borg, M.J., **Jesus: A New Vision,** 44.

4. Erikson, E., **Identity Youth And Crisis** (New York: W.W. Norton And Co., 1968).

5. Neugarten, B.L., Havighurst, R.J. & Tobin, S.S., "Personality And Patterns Of Aging," in B.L. Neugarten (Ed.) **Middle Age And Aging** (Chicago: University Of Chicago Press, 1968).

6. Kubler-Ross, E., **On Death And Dying** (New York: Macmillan, 1969).

13. Dare To Be A Christian With Your Mind, Heart And Feet

1. This **20/20** segment was aired in mid-1992. The program looked at the loneliness and isolation of gay children. It pointed out very wisely that a child with some other isolating life issue can at least go back to a home each night for comfort, solace and love; but that in many homes, this is not true for gay children. As a psychologist,

I know that the total lack of acceptance anywhere in a child's life would be enough to nurture suicide. As a Christian, I find this total lack of acceptance of a human child to be purely evil.

2. See Note Three in the Preface.

3. Booth, L., **When God Becomes A Drug: Breaking The Chains Of Religious Addiction And Abuse** (Los Angeles: Jeremy P. Tarcher, Inc., 1991).

4. Arterborn, S. & Felton, J., **Toxic Faith: Understanding And Overcoming Religious Addiction** (Nashville: Thomas Oliver Nelson, 1991).

5. Friel, J.C. & Friel, L.D., **Adult Children: The Secrets Of Dysfunctional Families** (Deerfield Beach, FL: Health Communications, 1988).

6. Friel, J.C. & Friel, L.D., **An Adult Child's Guide To What's "Normal"** (Deerfield Beach, FL: Health Communications, Inc., 1990).

14. To Think And Hope

1. Novak, M., **Belief And Unbelief: A Philosophy Of Self-Knowledge** (New York: Macmillan, 1965).

2. Allen, M.S., "Religious Leaders Seek Ways To End Racism," *Minneapolis Star Tribune*, June 22, 1992.

About the Author

John C. Friel, Ph.D., and his wife, Linda, are psychologists in private practice in St. Paul, Minnesota, where they specialize in working with adults who grew up in traumatic families. He is the national director of the Friel Lifeworks Clinics, an intensive, short-term treatment program for the family-of-origin causes of depression, addiction, relationship pain and related emotional issues. The clinics are offered in St. Paul and several other major U.S. cities.

John is also Adjunct Associate Professor of Psychology at St. Mary's College Graduate Institute in Minneapolis. He teaches continuing education classes for school personnel through the University of St. Thomas in St. Paul. He earned his B.A. in psychology from the University of San Francisco in 1969 and his Ph.D. in psychology from West Virginia University in 1976.

John is an internationally recognized trainer, speaker and consultant in the areas of family systems, addictions, men's issues, stress and religious abuse. He has consulted with a wide range of hospitals, government agencies, the military, treatment centers, colleges and universities, corporations, small businesses, law firms and medical practices throughout the United States, Canada and England.

He is the author of *The Grown-Up Man: Heroes, Healing, Honor, Hurt, Hope* and the co-author with Linda Friel of the two national bestsellers, *Adult Children: The Secrets Of Dysfunctional Families* and *An Adult Child's Guide To What's "Normal."*

Inquiries can be sent to John or Linda at:

Friel & Associates/Lifeworks
4176 N. Lexington Avenue
Shoreview, MN 55126
(612) 482-7982

INDEX